SPIRITUAL PURSUIT

Thirty One Day Journey

RICHARD B. SIMMONS

Published by LBFWorld Publishing
Houston, Tx

SPIRITUAL PURSUIT 31 DAY JOURNEY
Copyright © 2017 by Richard B. Simmons
PO Box 1198
Porter, Tx 77365
richardbsimmons.com

This book or parts thereof may not be reproduced in any form, stored in a retrieval system, or transmitted in any form by any means— electronic, mechanical, photocopy, recording, or otherwise— without prior written permission of the publisher, except as provided by United States of America copyright law.

SPIRITUAL PURSUIT 31 DAY JOURNEY
ISBN 978-1-946430-02-1

Printed in USA by LBFWorld Publishing
PO Box 1198
Porter, Tx 77365
LBFPublishing.com

Spiritual Pursuit 31 Day Journey by Richard B Simmons
Published by LBFPublishing
PO Box 1198
Porter, Texas 77365
www.LBFPublishing.com

Many of the LBFPublishing products are available at special discounts for bulk purchase for sales promotions, fund-raising, and educational needs. For details, contact LBFPublishing, PO Box 1198, Porter, Texas 77365, or eMail at info@lbfpublishing.com

Unless otherwise noted, all Scripture quotations are taken from the Holy Bible, New King James Version. **NKJV** Scripture taken from the New King James Version®. Copyright © 1982 by Thomas Nelson. Used by permission. All rights reserved.

Scripture quotations marked AMPC are from the Amplified Bible, Classic Edition. Copyright © 1954, 1958, 1962, 1964, 1965, 1987 by The Lockman Foundation. Used by permission.

Cover design by Richard B Simmons
Copyright © 2017 by Richard B Simmons
All rights reserved Visit the author's websites at richardbsimmons.com and http://spiritualpursuit.com/.

Library of Congress Cataloging-in-Publication Data: An application to register this book for cataloging has been submitted to the Library of Congress.

International Standard Book Number: 978-1-946430-02-1

While the author has made every effort to provide accurate information at the time of publication, neither the publisher nor the author assumes any responsibility for errors or for changes that occur after publication.

Dedication

I dedicate Spiritual Pursuit 31 Day Journey to my spiritual mother Mama Mig (Marjorie Bodine) a faithful handmaiden of the Lord.

Thank you for your love, and the many times of tremendous prayer, impartations, and encouragement. You were a truly unique, wondrous and an astonishing representation of Jesus Christ and used mightly by The Holy Spirit. You had a relationship with Jesus Christ and The Holy Spirit I have seen in very few on this earth.

You always taught the importance of not grieving the Holy Spirit but drawing closer, and the importance of letting go and letting God. After 92 years here on earth, your life sacrifice has rendered immeasurable fruit in the Kingdom! I am thankful you are now in the cloud of witnesses cheering us onward.

You impacted my life in so many ways for His glory. May this book reflect much of what you imparted over the years.

Table of Contents

Dedication...5
Table of Contents..6
Acknowledgements..8
Introduction...9
GOD IS CLOSER TO YOU THAN YOUR BREATH.....11
ALWAYS FORWARD NEVER BACK 15
HAVE COURAGE AND ACCEPT YES TRULY BELIEVE...19
DELIVERANCE, HEALING AND CLEANSING ARE YOURS 25
THE CORE OF FAITH...31
DOUBT AND UNBELIEF BLOCKS GOD'S POWER ...41
WHAT ARE YOU FOCUSED ON? 47
A NEW FAITH..53
HE CAME AND BROUGHT THE NEW COVENANT. 59
A HEALING BECOMES MANIFESTED...................71
BE AWARE OF THE HOUR......................................75
DARE TO BELIEVE AND RECEIVE FROM GOD......79
THE AUTHORITY AND POWER OF THE BLOOD OF JESUS..83
LIBERATION FROM FEAR......................................91
FAITH-NOT SOULISH FEELINGS 97
YOU ARE AN EPISTLE OF CHRIST......................101

PEACE AND HOPE	105
GOD IS WITH YOU	109
EXPERIENCE HIS JOY	113
SONSHIP	117
ALIVE TO GOD	123
WHAT DOES IT MEAN TO BELIEVE?	127
GOD IS NEAR	133
WHAT IS YOUR MOTIVE?	137
PRAYING IN THE SPIRIT	141
DESIRE GREATER WISDOM	145
THE POWER OF FAITH	149
THE GIFT OF FAITH	153
THE BAPTISM IN THE SPIRIT	157

Acknowledgements

Father God, Jesus Christ & The Holy Spirit – Thank you for your mercy, grace and fresh breath of Heaven, and never ending direction and guidance.

"Mom" Cynthia A Cox – Thank you for your never ending love and continued endless help with the book proofings, editing, and so much more. I am very thankful for your love, heart and help. You have always and will always be my hero .

"Mama Mig" Marjorie Bodine – To have had a spiritual mother like you was Gods divine plan. You helped shape my spiritual life tremendously. You finally got it through to me "Let go and Let God". I am looking forward to seeing you again in Heaven. You gave God 92 years of selfless obedient service.

Brian Shepherd – One words sums it up dedicated. Thank you for your dedication to the Lords work, and everything you do for me, the ministry, and the many people being touched through your love and gift of restoration. You are a blessing from the Lord a great pastor, teacher, spiritual son, mighty man of God, and servant.

Catherine Storing – Wow our divine meeting took me from prophetic words to come over my life to actually writing this book; my second book!! You are a great teacher. You truly brought forth a greater confidence in me and my desire to write and share with others how God has delivered for His glory and my growth. Thank you for you awesome: Confidence Unchained Ministry!! May God continue to use you and bring you forth to the people assigned to you. Amen

Introduction

Dear Friend,

God desires to introduce you and a whole generation of believers and new believers to the precious Holy Spirit. The word for this end time season is for the body of Christ to come to know the Holy Spirit and grow to a deeper place in the kingdom of God. The Holy Spirit will open up areas of understanding that no man could ever lead you to. He will teach you everything and more!

"These things I have spoken to you while being present with you. But the Helper, the Holy Spirit, whom the Father will send in My name, He will teach you all things, and bring to your remembrance all things that I said to you. -John 14:25-26

I truly believe He has brought you to this 31-day journey and that your reading this right now is no coincidence.

"But it was to us that God revealed these things by his Spirit. For his, Spirit searches out everything and shows us God's deep secrets." - 1 Corinthians 2: 10

The Holy Spirit has divine insight to the mind of God, and He distributes those secrets and mysteries as you draw close and near and position yourself to hear that small still voice speaking to you. I pray that this 31-day journey will give you inspiration, impartation and a whole new relationship with the Lord.

DAY ONE

GOD IS CLOSER TO YOU THAN YOUR BREATH

"Behold, the virgin shall be with child and give birth to a Son, and they shall call His name Immanuel"— which, when translated, means, "God with us."
Matthew 1:23 AMP

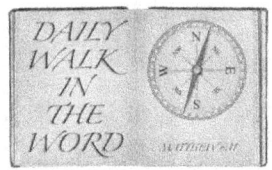

Matthew 1:18-25 and Philippians 2:5-11

Day One

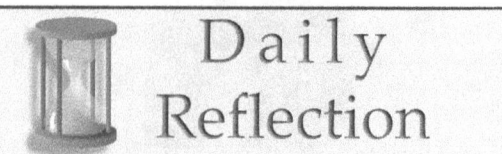

Now the birth of Jesus Christ was as follows:

After His mother, Mary was betrothed (engaged) to Joseph, before they came together, she was found pregnant with a child of the Holy Spirit. Then Joseph her soon to be husband, being a just man, and not wanting to make her a public example, was minded to put her away secretly.

But while he thought about these things, behold, an angel of the Lord appeared to him in a dream, saying, "Joseph, son of David, do not be afraid to take to you Mary your wife, for that which is conceived in her is of the Holy Spirit. And she will bring forth a Son, and you shall call His name Jesus, for He will save His people from their sins." - Matthew 1:20-21

So all this was done that it might be fulfilled which was spoken by the Lord through the prophet, saying:

Spiritual Pursuit

"Behold, the virgin shall be with child, and bear a Son, and they shall call His name Immanuel," when translated, "God with us." -Matthew 1:23

Then Joseph was awoken from sleep, as the angel of the Lord commanded him and took him his wife, and did not know her till she had brought forth her firstborn Son. And they called His name Jesus. -Matthew 1:24-25

Desire that this mind is in you which was also in Christ Jesus, who, being in the form of God, did not consider it robbery to be equal with God, but made Himself of no reputation, taking on the form of a bondservant, and coming to this earth in the likeness of men. And being found in appearance as a man, He humbled Himself and became obedient to the point of death, even the death on the cross at Calvary.

Therefore God also has highly exalted Him and given Him the name which is above every name, at the name of Jesus every knee shall bow, of those in heaven, and of those on earth, and of those under the earth, and that every tongue should confess that Jesus Christ is Lord, to the glory of God the Father.

Day One

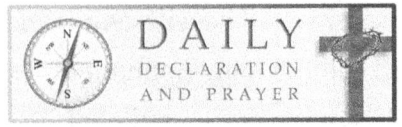

Father in Jesus name I Desire that this mind which is in Christ Jesus be also in me. Today I declare and decree in Jesus name I have the mind of Christ Jesus, Lord I ask you to reveal anything in me that opposes or resists the kingdom of Heaven that I may place it at the altar and come closer to you and have more of the mind of Christ Jesus. I thank you in Jesus name. Amen

DAY TWO

ALWAYS FORWARD NEVER BACK

As newborn babes, desire the pure milk of the word,
that you may grow thereby.
1 Peter 2:2

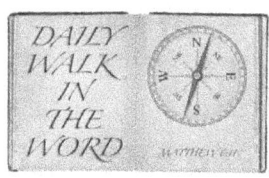

1 Peter 1:13-2:5

Day Two

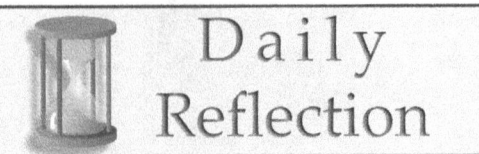
Daily Reflection

Many people do not like the trials and tribulations in the Christian walk, but these are the strengthening places of advancement in our walk our promotions or demotions. The walk of a Christian was never promised to be easy, but His glory increases in our life as we go through and conquer the trials and tribulations. Yes, pass the test!

These trials and tribulations happen to reconstruct or rebuild us to who God has called us to be for His plans and purposes. These will not come at the most opportune times or convenient situations, but He will never leave you nor forsake you! Yes, He is our ever present help in time of need.

What am I saying? He is nearby, and easy to find! Ask, Seek, and Knock! He will open the door for you, but until the door opens keep knocking as His small child.

When you think you have gone far enough, can't handle anymore, and so on remember to "count it all joy" and press forward!

Spiritual Pursuit

Take a quick look at Matthew 11:29 -
Take My yoke upon you and learn from Me, for I am gentle and lowly in heart, and you will find rest for your souls. -You will find rest!

The Holy Spirit was sent by Jesus and has come to show up in highly powerful ways to advance the kingdom through you! This means we must take the things off of our plate that doesn't belong there! They are robbing us of our time with Him and hindering your advancement in the Kingdom for His Glory.

When you are obedient and submit to The Holy Spirit's direction which comes at a significant cost. A mighty anointed river will flow through you of God's great glory! The anointing of the oil coming forth will bring life to the deadest thing, even water in your driest desert.

"Be strong" because in your weakness He is your strength!

Day Two

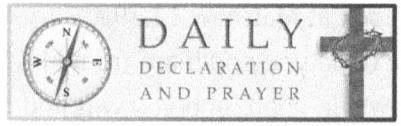

God wants to pour His glory out through me, and will because I choose to submit to the Holy Spirit, and empty my plate of everything not of God's perfect will in my life for today!

DAY THREE

HAVE COURAGE AND ACCEPT YES TRULY BELIEVE

As it is written, "I have made you a father of many nations."
Romans 4:17

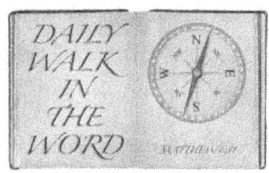

Genesis 15:3-6; 18:9-15

Day Three

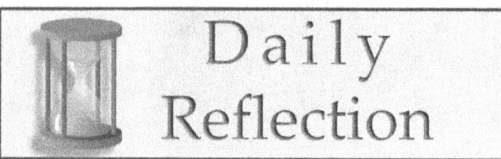

We're looking at Sarah and Abraham, both of their bodies were almost dead. Abraham said to God " now " look at this "God has made me a father of many nations, and there is no hope of a son according to the natural law, no hope whatsoever."

So here God is speaking to Abraham and is telling him "I have made you a father of many nations, " but there's a little problem with this and you may ask what that problem is? The problem is Abraham at this point does not have a son, and he is of an ancient age.

Everything Abraham and Sarah had been facing over the past 20 years completely contradict what is being said in fact the conditions have continued worsening, and it looks utterly hopeless, but God. Let us never forget and always remember that God is not a liar. What He says will come to pass in His perfect time, not ours.

How long have you been standing on the promises of God? Maybe some hopes have not come to pass yet. So here comes that old lying voice of the devil that says a

Spiritual Pursuit

multitude of things to you all which our deceptions yes flat out lies purposed to get you off of God's perfect plan for your life.

You know what I'm talking about with his lies. The devil will say something like this, God made you a promise but He failed you, or you're not important to God, and it will never happen for you. The reality is the devil is a liar, and he came to steal, kill and destroy.

The reality is that as a true believer and follower of Jesus Christ you are saved through Jesus Christ and His shed blood, and if you're living life as the Bible directs us and being led by the Holy Spirit you are saved, and you're blessed.

Let us look at the faithfulness of Abraham as we see in Galatians chapter 3:9. Abraham was called a friend of God. Abraham had great faith, in fact, he believed God for 25 years when everything continued to get worse around him daily.

If we will trust and believe God the way Abraham did, we begin to enter such a fantastic relationship with God that is seldom seen in this world, and especially here in America. He will start transforming us into people who truly walk in the relationship, favor, and a supernatural lifestyle of the most high God.

Day Three

When we look in the book of Hebrews 11:6 we see that God is And that He is a rewarder of those who diligently seek him.

God is more real than anything that exists on this earth. God is light and life and complete truth. Remember He is not a God to lie. Let us stay focused on the truth and not listen to the lies of the devil which are meant to kill, steal and destroy. Yes, that's his plan to pull us right off of God's perfect plan to increase and prosper us.

God never fails, and He only wants a man to believe. When the person believes in his heart at that point man will never fail!

Abraham had to look past the natural through the lens of faith, belief and had to know God was going to turn this thing around and make it right. Abraham knew that God is the reality. More real than anything in his natural life. He was aware that God was closer than his breath.

Look in the book of Romans 4:17 we see, " God... gives life to the dead and calls those things which do not exist as though they did."

What we see next of course is a test that's part of our Christian walk. So God tested Abraham and Sarah. Yes,

Spiritual Pursuit

they walked through fire, God knows how to deal with us. As we pass those test. Then flows the blessings.

Always remember this there is no lack with God and therefore no lack for those who trust God. We must get zeroed in on the perfect will of God in our lives. God can turn any situation around and bring peace in the most chaotic places.

Abraham was having a blast he embraced the opportunities of testing and the more God dealt with him and tested him the more he rejoiced and increased.

Let's take a look at Romans 4:19-20.

And not being weak in faith, he did not consider his body, already dead (since he was about a hundred years old), and the deadness of Sarah's womb. He did not waver at the promise of God through unbelief but was strengthened in faith, giving glory to God.

God is all-knowing; let us remember He has a plan and a purpose for your life that was set before the foundations of the earth before you ever entered your mother's womb. He has made a way where naturally there is no way. Take a look at Jeremiah 29:11-14.

Day Three

Now here's the question, are you going dare to trust God and see His fullness manifest in your life?

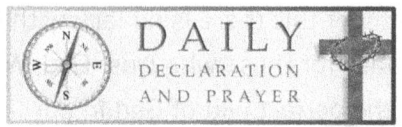

God, I trust you through my testings, and as I go through tests, I realize you'll show me what you made me in you, and reveal to me your greater plan for my life.

DAY FOUR

DELIVERANCE, HEALING AND CLEANSING ARE YOURS

If you bring your gift to the altar, and there remember that your brother has something against you, leave your gift there before the altar, and go your way. First be reconciled to your brother, and then come and offer your gift.
Matthew 5:23-24

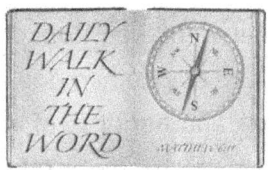

Matthew 5:13-26

Day Four

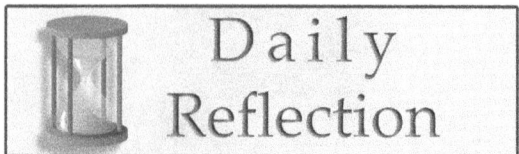
Daily Reflection

I will say this. It just takes one touch from the King.

Going back many years when my father Ed was in Hermann Hospital he had fallen away from his walk with Jesus Christ and had succumbed to tremendous illness.

As he laid there on his deathbed, he describes at a later time the following to me. He began to feel himself being pulled into the mattress downward he said.

Satan had come to take him to hell, But Jesus Christ appeared to him. The Lord Jesus said to him "you can go straight to hell or come back and fix what you've done." He apparently made the right choice and chose to return in love and repair the offenses.

One of the great miracles that came from this was the fact that he had been delivered from drinking a fifth of vodka a day. From the day he had one touch from the King, he never drank another drop of alcohol in his life; nor, did he ever have any desire or relapses. He was genuinely delivered.

Spiritual Pursuit

Jesus Christ is the healer of the broken hearted, and the deliver of the captive yes that's right he takes the very worst of each of us and sets us free if we will allow him to. Take a look here at Isaiah 61.

Isaiah 61:1 -The Good News of Salvation

The Spirit of the Lord God is upon Me,
Because the Lord has anointed Me
To preach good tidings to the poor;
He has sent Me to heal the brokenhearted,
To proclaim liberty to the captives,
And the opening of the prison to those who are bound;

The truth of the gospel of Jesus Christ is that it breaks us free from your bondage and brings us into a place of liberty, and in my dad's case, Jesus restored the health of his body. After this experience, my father's salvation and Kingdom impact were back on track.

Through the years my father had come into a tremendous amount of pain and anger which the enemy utilized to get in and begin a dark downward spiral.

One thing we need to understand is that God can never bless us walking around with hard hearts, with unforgiveness and a critical spirit.

Day Four

*Remember, if you do not forgive, you will not be forgiven. Take a look at Mark 11:26.

The very moment we allow Jesus to cleanse us the Spirit of God Will fall upon us.

If you are yearning for healing in your life and it has not manifested, take a look in your heart and see if you were harboring any anger, Hate, rage, or forgiveness and so on.

If you are this is hindering your healing!

But not to worry the Bible tells us that if we forgive the Lord will forgive us. So forgive those who've hurt you, wounded you or rejected you whatever the case may be, it's okay, just release them to The Lord.

Repent for your unforgiveness, and ask the Lord to forgive you. Now when you have done this from your heart, the Lord has forgiven you. The blood of Jesus Christ cleanses and covers you. Merely believe now and receive the fullness of His love and deliverance.

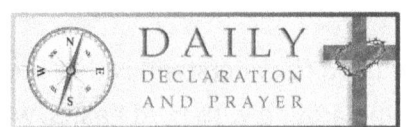

Spiritual Pursuit

Father God in Jesus name I choose to surrender to you and forgive. I repent for every sin in my life and ask you to forgive me. I desire to tune into you as you are the author and finisher of my Faith. You're my healer, and my deliver my ever present help in time of need and today I receive your love, healing and cleansing through the blood of Jesus Christ.

DAY FIVE

THE CORE OF FAITH

For in [the gospel of Christ] the righteousness of God is revealed from faith to faith; as it is written, "The just shall live by faith." Romans 1:17

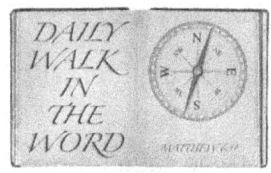

Romans 1:5-20

Day Five

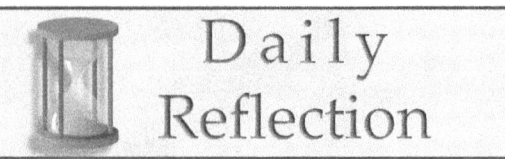
Daily Reflection

A lot of people ask what exactly faith is?

Well, that's a great question. Faith is the very fullness, the vast nature of God Almighty. Faith is the Bible. Faith is the fullness of the Word of God. Faith is a very unfathomable place inside of you, a very deep place that taps into a flow that is God.

This deeply rooted deposit moves through your body to every molecule, cell, and fiber of your being. As your faith is coming up to higher levels, you begin to notice that your life, your mind, your whole nature begins to go through a paradigm shift. Yes, at this point you're starting to live a deep-rooted life of faith.

We now look at this as the gift of faith at this point.

Why is it important to be caught up in high faith, to move with high confidence? Well, the reason is just this extraordinary. It's because this is what's necessary to enter into a deep, glorious place with God. Yes, to be taken up in the glory is done by faith.

Spiritual Pursuit

Faith is the very thing of knowing a profound personal presence that resides in you—that profound personal presence that is bringing the paradigm shift or change in you, as some would say from glory to glory, mountain to mountain, and through the valley.

We go through these things and grow until we get into this mysterious place or actually in an entirely dependent relationship filled walk with God.

You say what does that look like? It looks like this. God begins to speak and communicate to us. In fact, He speaks to us and gives us communications that come through the Holy Spirit, and it's for His glory.

God never designed us just to exist and be. God intended for us to excel in Him, be fruitful and multiply. God desires us to have so much more than we have right now. He designed us to have a fullness because He gets glory for it.

In Hebrews 11:1, the truth in His Word says this— "the substance of things hoped for, the evidence of things not seen." We've got to stay focused on faith daily yes on Jesus Christ. Walk with a pang of hunger to go deeper, and deeper, and deeper into greater faith and confidence

Day Five

ultimately surrendering to the Spirit of God in complete trust and surrender.

When we look in the Word of God, we see so many Truths that draw us close to faith because as we said earlier, faith is the living Word of God.

Looking at Psalms 90:2, we see it says, from everlasting to everlasting. And as we talked about earlier in Hebrews 11:1, we know one thing. The Word of God tells us the Truth and this Truth is in Hebrews 11:1—faith is the substance and the evidence is the things not seen.

Let's take a minute and reflect upon that. Faith is the material. Looking at that word in Hebrews 11:1 substance equals faith.

So many times, we look at specific things that people do.

Let's take this example: ladies can take tomatoes, onions, ground beef and great things that they would utilize to prepare an excellent meal. Why are they able to make this wonderful meal? Well, sure, they have the experience or gifting to cook! But they also have the materials—the tomatoes, the onions, the ground beef, the things necessary, the materials if you will.

Spiritual Pursuit

Likewise, with men. Some men enjoy working on their vehicles. I do. They have wrenches; they have ratchets, they have air impact equipment. It makes this job of working on the car work well. Why? Well, again, they have the materials necessary—the tools, they have the new parts to replace the parts that are worn out or broken. So, ultimately, they have the materials as well, whether you are a lady or a man, whether you like to be in the kitchen or working under the hood. It's not unique to a gender, but these are some examples. The point we were making there is these people had the materials they needed to complete the task.

Now, looking at this, we'll go back and look into the very beginning—Genesis. We see God did something very miraculous. Many things, in fact, but today we are focusing on this. God, without any materials whatsoever, spoke from his mouth and what came forth was this world and the many beautiful, miraculous things that we see daily.

God did this with no materials there. God did this by merely speaking, and it formed.

As you see in the Bible in the book of Genesis, it's written there. What happened? The very truth written in the Bible was spoken, and He called it into being. How

Day Five

did he do this? -Because He's God. He's the creator, and He's the very force behind this.

We operate with the same truths today—the facts that are written in the Bible, the basic instructions before leaving earth.

We're told if you lack any good thing to ask—that includes knowledge, wisdom, discernment and so much more—in this case, He used knowledge and that knowledge we have, the knowledge that we are born again and saved by Jesus Christ.

Let's take a moment and reflect on 1 Peter 1:23, "Having been born again, not of corruptible seed but incorruptible, through the Word of God which lives and abides forever." What do we see here? -That inside of you is the fullness of hope. Inside of you is something much bigger and more powerful than yourself, in fact, something stronger than anything on this earth.

When you became a new creation of God, and Jesus Christ saves you, faith begins to work in you like a mustard seed. We need to have great audacity when it comes to faith. We need to take ourselves and get bold and just throw ourselves in the situations, being led by faith because God's going to meet us there. God has a

Spiritual Pursuit

divine plan that's filled with so much power, filled with omnipotence, in fact.

In the Word of God in Mark 9:23, He says, "If you can believe, all things are possible to him who believes." Look at what he says there—if you can believe. Then, He goes on to say; all things are possible to him who believes.

Family, today I know, your belief is coming to a new level. He's asking you here if you believe. I think this should be, do you choose to believe? So many people look at their surroundings today, and they don't see a whole lot of individuals that are manifesting the fullness of God in their churches, office places, shopping malls, grocery stores, or even hospitals. But it's possible if we believe. It's entirely possible for this full power of God to manifest in each of our lives in more significant ways that have ever happened before.

Daily, we need to believe, and we need to jump out into greater faith. If we do this, we will always be moving forward in great victory. You say why? —Because the truth of the matter is, God knows no defeat, and the fullness of God is faith; therefore, faith knows no loss or defeat.

Day Five

We must delve into the Word of God like never before. Daily, we must eat the Word in such a way that it fills us with greater faith. God wants us to have an incredibly clear understanding of what faith is. Faith is God's plan, and it is divine. Faith is the very thing that brings you to the doors that are opened by God that you may enter, but you must have an open door.

It's impossible to get into a door that's locked or closed. God is the one who opens the doors and faith will take us to that open door. This faith is the fullness of God. He prepares us that when we arrive at that open door, we are ready to step in and go forth in the fullness of what He has for us—the fullness of His promises.

We will find significant manifestations of His power in Jesus Christ. The reality is, it's impossible for us to face and deal with the enemy, conquering him, because in 1 John 4:4, the Word of God says, "He who is in you is greater than he who is in the world."

Having a lifestyle of faith— that means living it, not a religious aspect of relationship—gives us a credibility that's divine in nature, for this is where we find Jesus Christ manifested in each of our lives, to the fullness of the truth in the Bible.

Spiritual Pursuit

Remember this, we gain much knowledge through the Word of God, and we know that God is the one who changes each of us through Jesus Christ and The Holy Spirit.

He takes away everything that causes us to fail in the past—weakness, fear, every inability. All the things that cause us to fail are now a thing of the past because we are filled with great faith.

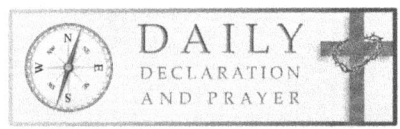

Father God, in Jesus Name, I thank you for the faith that has incredible "dunamis" power to make me what you want me to be, Lord God. God, I know, I've got to be ready to step in to that door when you bring me to it and it's open. And today, Lord, as you prepare me to step forward and be ready when the door opens, to step into the fullness of your perfect plan, and Father, to help me believe the totality of your truth in the Bible In Jesus mighty name!

DAY SIX

DOUBT AND UNBELIEF BLOCKS GOD'S POWER

Now He did not do many mighty works there because
of their unbelief.
Matthew 13:58

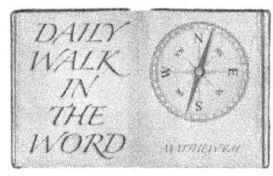

Hebrews 3:8-19

Day Six

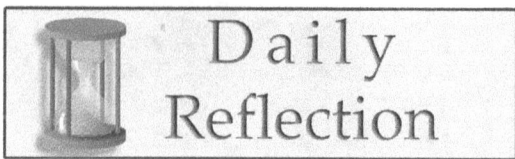
Daily Reflection

Unbelief hinders the power of God! The Holy Spirit wants us to fully comprehend that nothing can interfere with the perfect blessing except for us, and that is through unbelief.

Unbelief is a killer; it's a complete hindrance. If we let go and let God and allow the Holy Spirit to have His way in our lives, we will find amazing things unfolding every day and all the time. But there's something that's got to take place before that. And it's something that many people are challenged with. That is our human reasoning.

We must choose to discard and get rid of human reasoning entirely. All these plans we make, we got to cut those things loose, throw them in the trash, and be done with them. We've got to live life by the Holy Spirit, and that involves letting go and letting God and be led by the Spirit of God.

Belief is critical, and it's essential, and without it, it's impossible to please God.

Spiritual Pursuit

The Spirit of God wants to bring great focus to truths in our lives, but we must not fight Him. We must yield our lives to His plan—His perfect divine plan. When we find ourselves yielding to Him and spending time with Him, we see Him unfolding great and mighty things. Divine plans, in fact.

He wants to bring forth many hidden things for each of us, many truths that aren't known on this earth. This involves a tremendous belief in the Bible.

So many people today go around holding the Bible in some sort of religious fashion. There is a particular pride and arrogance that's behind it. But how many actually believe the Word of God, not just quote it?

We must have the Word of God in us. It must be a part of us. It must be alive in the molecules, cells, fibers or our body. Meaning, we are living it, and it's a part of us, not just religiously quoting to be seen as somebody greater or mightier.

There's so much truth in the Word, but it has to be alive in our hearts. Many people quote 1 John 4:4, "He who is in you is greater than he who is in the world." But I ask you something. As you say this Scripture, is this really taking place in your life? Can you go to a demonized

Day Six

person and can they remain in your presence or do they have to get out of there?

We've got to be greater than demonic influence—greater than demons. We've got to be greater than sickness, illness, infirmities, diseases. We've got to be able to stand on the Word of God and face the facts of many difficulties that come with us in this life. It brings back so many times of ministering, but one specifically took place as I was ministering to a group of youth in Houston, Texas. So, as I was going around and ministering to the youth, I would just pass by certain young people, and they would begin to manifest the demons. I literally had to lead thru deliverance and get them set free.

I've seen similar things unfold in Cape Town, South Africa. Just being in their very presence, and they would begin to froth at the mouth, stiffened up like a board and fall backward. This is what we're speaking of.

In Hebrews 11:1, the Word of God says that faith is the substance of things hoped for. Remember something as we talked about earlier in this devotional, faith is the Word; faith is God. The Word of God has got to be in us. The Word of God is life and power. And God ultimately requires and wants us to fully and unconditionally believe because it's impossible to please him if we don't

Spiritual Pursuit

believe. It boils down to this believe and receive in His perfect timing.

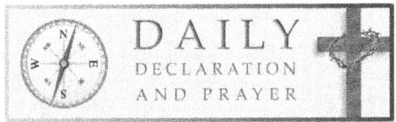

Father God, nothing in this world can stand against me because I choose to fully believe you Lord. It is the total truth and is written in 1 John 4:4, that "He who is in me is greater than he who is in the world". I declare this today and fully believe and receive, in Jesus Name.

DAY SEVEN

WHAT ARE YOU FOCUSED ON?

And the prayer of faith will save the sick, and the Lord will raise him up.
-James 5:15

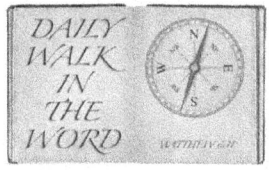

James 5:13-20

Day Seven

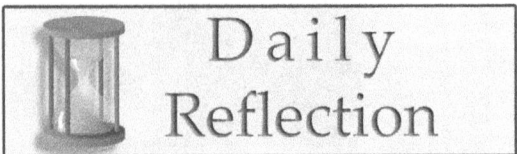
Daily Reflection

Years ago, as a child, I recalled being at a hospital. As the doctor called my family in, saying, my father Ed would die within 24 hours, something in the depth of me could not believe or receive that. Why should I? I had seen so many miracles so far.

That day was a game-changer in my place of belief in the supernatural, miraculous healing of the highest God. My father's sister named Bonnie who is a Spirit-filled believer was called along with other family members to report immediately to Hermann Hospital in Houston, Texas. She arrived at the hospital and sat with the other family members in the lobby. She encountered another woman in the waiting area. Bonnie had never met this woman before. It was clearly a divine encounter with the Lord.

The two of them agreed to pray for my father. The importance of this brings us to the connection in the book of James 5:14-15. It says, "Is anyone among you sick? Let them call for the elders of the church. Let them pray over him anointing him with oil in the name of the

Spiritual Pursuit

Lord." And in verse 15, it goes on to say, "And the prayer of faith will save the sick, and the Lord would raise him up, and if he committed sins, he will be forgiven."

That day, my father sat there on the death bed on the brink of mortality. I had seen many other people come and pray for him, but they seemed, honestly, to be the traditional powerless prayers. You know the prayers that come in and say, "I'm here; I'm compassionate" but lacking true faith and belief in the supernatural healing. Those prayers are really lacking faith and confidence in the Lords promises and, the power of the Holy Spirit, to change the situation in front of them.

As they went in to pray, here I was a young man at that age of eleven years old, looking into the intensive care unit window of his room. And I see a multidimensional supernatural blue light come out. Not long after that, Aunt Bonnie and this unknown woman come out from the room, and the woman looks into my eyes as I feel something looking literally into me through my eye gates into my soul. She says to me, "Son, your father is gonna be just fine. He's surrounded by the angels of the Lord." I honestly believe this lady was an angel on assignment from the Lord.

I tell you this today to say faith was set upon the Lord doing the work. But I also said this to say that in James

Day Seven

5:14-15, we see in verse 15, it says, "The prayer of faith will save the sick, and the Lord will raise him up, and if he has committed sins, he will be forgiven." Aunt Bonnie shared with me sometime later that Jesus walked off that elevator with her and told her the prayer to pray.

That day was he not only restored and pardoned from death; he was delivered from the evil one by the King of kings yes the Lord of lords none other than Jesus Christ.

My encouragement to you today is this, let us not gaze upon the people who are dying in the situation that's there. Let us affix our eyes and belief to the Lord Jesus Christ. I know that His truth sets them free. Let us not partake in prayers that are filled with unbelief. It's Jesus Christ that makes us whole as He did with my father, Ed.

Spiritual Pursuit

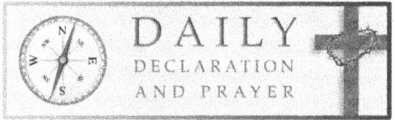

Father God, in Jesus Name, help me to keep my eyes off of the condition or symptoms that are present naturally, but to set my eyes on you, Lord, that I would be able to truly pray the prayer of faith. There's truly only one place for me to look for the supernatural healing and deliverance, Lord. And that is in you, Jesus.

DAY EIGHT

A NEW FAITH

Where is your faith?
Luke 8:25

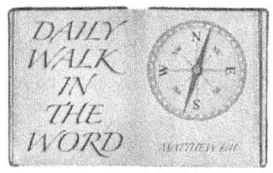

Luke 8:22-39

Day Eight

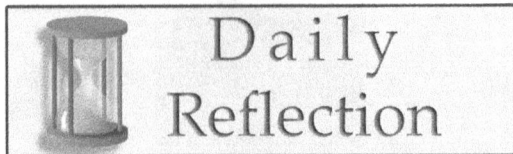
Daily Reflection

Paul the Apostle spoke of two different types of Christians—obedient Christians and disobedient Christians—those who choose to follow the Lord and the Holy Spirit to a higher place and those that live in a rebellious state. Daily, we're progressing and moving forward, or we're backsliding. The obedient Christian/the believer always obeys God when God first speaks, not on the second, third or fourth time, but initially when God speaks. These are the people the Lord wants to use and will use to make world changes. These are the people that are going to impact nations and shake the very place of this world with the kingdom of God.

We can't go around talking about things that we've not experienced. This is why many people need to understand that we go through mountains and valleys. We go through these times to learn. We go through these times that we would gain experience and it's a process of training for us as well. We have got to go through a process of breaking that God can take us to deeper depths.

Spiritual Pursuit

In Psalm 34:18, the Word of God says, The Lord is near to those who have a broken heart. We must go through a place of breaking to come to brokenness for God to actually be able to use us to reach those who are lost and broken. With this comes a greater confidence in God, comes a greater faith in God. In Romans 10:17, the Word of God says that faith comes by hearing and hearing by the Word of God. The Word of God creates such a deep place of faith—a faith that fills your molecules, the cells and the fibers of your very being; a faith that cannot be moved; a faith that never gives up; a faith that never fails—for this very faith is the nature of God Almighty. So many times, we don't realize how great and generous the Father is, the Kingdom is.

One time, as I was flying to Costa Rica, the Lord begin to speak to me, sitting on a runway 22 at Houston George Bush Intercontinental Airport. He showed me to the right of the aircraft some fuel supply tanks. And He begins to speak to me, and He said, "Son, do you understand what those tanks do?" And I said, "Well, Lord, they provide fuel for the planes." And He said, "Yes," and He said, "My Kingdom is much greater." He said the supply is never-ending. One thing that God showed me that day was that the provision of heaven never runs dry. It can never be exhausted. You see, God is very much pleased when we seek Him for far greater when we're looking for Him for the impossible.

Day Eight

In Matthew 7:11, the Word of God says, If you then, being evil, know how to give good gifts to your children, how much more will your Father who is in heaven give good things to those who ask him?

God wants to show us so much more. He wants to demonstrate things that are miraculous in nature, that are uncommon and unseen, that He will be glorified. Many times in life, in our walk with God, we feel that we faced a wall. We think that we met a solid wall. However, we don't move or respond to our emotions. We don't walk by our feelings. When things are dark, when things are uncertain, we've got not to be moved by fear. We've got to have the highest confidence ever, and that assurance is in God Almighty. We've got to know that God is infallible and He is immeasurable. The fact is, the Word of God says He will never leave us nor forsake us. The Word of God declares that He is our ever present help in time of need.

Brothers and sisters, dear friends, we've got to have an unimaginable confidence to understand and believe that He will not and cannot fail us. If we operate out of feelings, we're operating out of the soul. Let us nevermore do that. That won't get us anyplace. That would bring us nowhere.

Spiritual Pursuit

However, when we stand upon the Word of God, we stand upon truth. The very point of standing on the Word of God and seeking Him brings us nearer to the Holy Spirit, and that very place is where God begins to bring profound revelation from heaven to the depths of us. Let us stop operating and reacting out of the passions and excitements of emotion and let us ascend into the fullness of the Lord God Almighty. Let us accept and receive the new kingdom that we've been born into and to a tremendous all-embracing new faith that God possesses for us today.

Day Eight

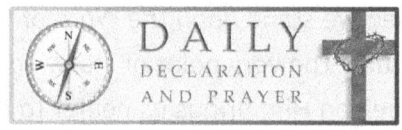

Father God, in Jesus Name, I am listening to your voice. Lord as your word and voice become clearer to me; I will do anything and everything you direct me to do. God, I ask you to confirm and make it clear that it is Your voice as your you said in John 10:27 "My sheep hear my voice, and I know them, and they follow me". I will step out and meet You Lord and respond to what you've told me to do. I choose to believe and walk by faith, not by sight. In Jesus name!

DAY NINE

HE CAME AND BROUGHT THE NEW COVENANT

This cup is the new covenant in My blood, which is shed for you.
Luke 22:20

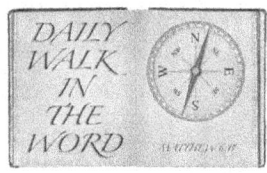

2 Corinthians 3:3-18

Day Nine

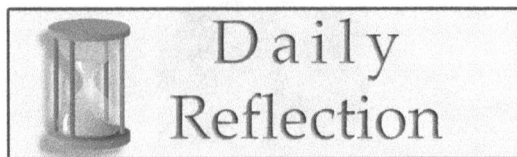

The Israelites were always in issues, consistently challenging Moses. You can only imagine Moses daily in his walk, having to deal with the consistent problems, until a fantastic day arrived—a day that Moses ascended yes Moses took a trail up that mountain, and God Almighty presented before him the Ten Commandments. As He did this, the very glory of God fell upon Moses.

I can only imagine the joy Moses felt as the glory was upon him, yearning to bring the two tablets of stone with the Ten Commandments written on them, down from the mountainside to the people. As Moses was glowing with the very glory of God that radiated from him. This was huge as Moses was bringing a new opportunity for Israel. If only they would obey, they would find new life in it. As grand as that was, it doesn't even begin to parallel to Jesus' coming to this earth and bringing us new life and a new covenant.

Looking at Moses, we see the very glory of Him that was found on the mountain of Sinai. But again, it has no comparison to the glory that was found on Pentecost.

Spiritual Pursuit

The fire certainly fell at Pentecost, and the New Covenant honestly came with Jesus, and there was the fulness of the Holy Spirit.

When we look at the Bible at Jeremiah 31:33, the Lord has delivered a new covenant, establishing his law in our minds and writing it on our hearts. Notice it says here, putting his law in our minds and writing it on our hearts. This new law He's referring to is the law of the Spirit of Life. The Holy Spirit of God arrives to deliver love and liberty, and as He does this, a new place in our heart begins, full of love and freedom.

In Hebrews 10:9, He takes away the first that He may establish the second. He's simply saying here that the ministry of death that was written and engraved on stones at one point is no longer. In verse 9, He becomes clear that Jesus came to establish the ministry of righteousness, worship, spirituality, holiness and this is achieved in a life with the Holy Spirit. We had to become Christ-like—ambassadors of Christ. In 2 Corinthians 3:3, we see, we have to become living epistles of Jesus Christ.

In 2004, God began to influence and impress in my life like never before. I was discovering new freedom, and a short time later I was baptized in the Holy Spirit. A unique perspective and a transformation came upon my life like never before. The new life in the Spirit was

Day Nine

flowing forward. The law, as they call it, did not bring this life, but rather, the Spirit of the Living God—the very Spirit that begins to pull me back, like I was in a slingshot, and send me forward into everything God had put in motion in my life.

As we begin this walk with God and realize the importance of Jesus Christ, coming as our Lord and Savior, and going through death, burial, resurrection, and ascension. Jesus was delivering the New Covenant; we understand that we don't live under the law anymore, but instead, we have been placed in a slingshot and are being prepared to be catapulted forward by His Spirit into the very narrow path He has called us to walk. That is if we will surrender, believe, and obey his voice.

In our new life in Jesus Christ, walking in the Spirit, let us never forget that Jesus Christ delivered us to a new covenant, to a place where we need to love and adore the very things that are true, that are pure, and that are of holiness.

In John 14:30, the ruler of this world is coming, and he has nothing in me. There's nothing greater than being filled with the Spirit of God, for this is the very thing the new covenant leads us to an excellent, new state only found in the new covenant with the baptism in Holy Spirit.

Spiritual Pursuit

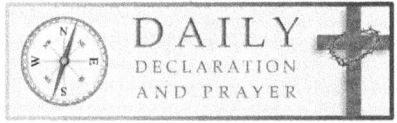

Father God, in Jesus Name, I thank you that I am daily being filled with more of Your Spirit and that He that is in me is greater than He who is in the world. Father, I declare, in Jesus Name, the further I am in the Spirit, the enemy has no residence in me. In Jesus name

DAY TEN

A SOLID PLAN FOR YOU

Be faithful until death, and I will give you the crown of life.
Revelation 2:10

Acts 6:1-7; Revelation 2:9-11

Day Ten

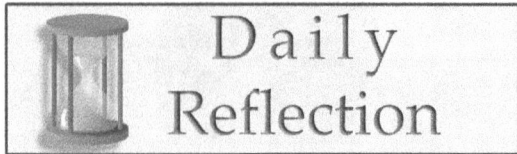
Daily Reflection

The twelve disciples instructed all the remaining disciples to go and find seven men that were to look after the administrative portion. These seven men were to be men with outstanding characters. They were to be men that have been filled with the Holy Spirit. Yes, these men were not superstars. They were ordinary common men and what separated them apart from the others was the very filling of the Holy Spirit that was within each of them. A man who is immersed and overflowing with the Holy Spirit operates on a whole different level that's not normal or usual to the average man.

As they were seeking, they made their choice of seven men that were established and placed to serve tables. The significant thing to observe here is that these seven men possess the spirit of excellence. They were filled with the Holy Spirit and they stayed committed and true in what they have been selected to do.

As they were serving in excellence and doing as they were appointed to do, God came upon the scene with a shift of orders for two of them— Steven and Philip. The

Spiritual Pursuit

fact is, Philip was overflowing in the Holy Spirit to such a point that anywhere he walked, revival went with him. You say what's the point here? It's pretty simple. Many times, men will make selections of people to serve in duties, and God comes forward after observing excellence and obedience and sets specific people's feet to a distinct responsibility of winning souls, with miracles, signs, and wonders following. Yes, a summons to do this every day as their mission. These are charged to the calling of the ministry.

A huge key I found on my walk is this: to walk in a place of complete humility and to be faithful to God's purpose and God's timing. As it was seen with William Seymour of the Azusa Street Revival, he was incredibly humble, truly faithful, and walked in a tremendous place of excellence, and God came and filled Seymour to overflowing with His precious Holy Spirit. In the best timing, God comes after reproving and transforms you into a vessel that has been chosen for Himself. In the appropriate timing and season, God will come and increase you to large, mighty places and to minister for His glory, for the purposes of healings, miracles, signs, wonders, and ultimately, salvations of souls. The reality is, to the man who is filled with the Holy Spirit, there is no failure—the man who is full of the abundance and overflowing power of the Holy Spirit who has extraordinary works wherever he goes.

Day Ten

Many times, people will say, "I just don't know if I catch the voice of God. I'm not sure if I can hear the voice of God." The truth is this, as you are filled with the abundance of the Holy Spirit, you will undoubtedly identify, recognize and listen to the voice of God.

Don't try to maneuver or shift out of God's timing or plan if you don't want to miss it. As you're walking through the times and seasons, be committed, be humble, walk-in completeness. You honestly have no idea, no clue what God Almighty can and will accomplish through you when you are filled with His precious Holy Spirit. When you are filled with the Holy Spirit of God, you will walk, minute by minute, day by day, in a place of being divinely guided, and directed by the Holy Spirit.

Spiritual Pursuit

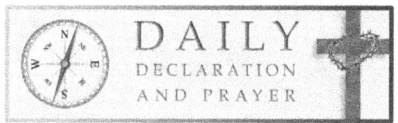

Father God, in Jesus' Name, I recognize I don't need to be the man with the greatest suit, the man with the most distinguished degree, or the man with the most wealth. I want to be the humble man—an abandoned man, the man who walks in a place of holiness, the man of submission. I pray today that You would take me to the places necessary to be this man, for Your glory and honor. In Jesus' Name, Amen!

DAY ELEVEN

A HEALING BECOMES MANIFESTED

Reality He Himself took our infirmities and bore our sicknesses.
Matthew 8:17

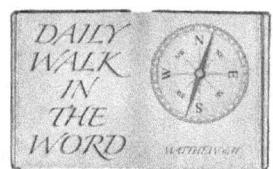

Isaiah 53:1-12

Day Eleven

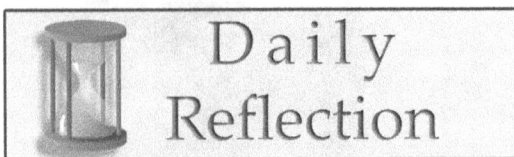
Daily Reflection

I want to share with you a fantastic story of a supernatural miracle in the healing that manifested through Jesus for an orphan young man in Honduras. This all took place when I was on a mission to the orphanage in LaCeiba, Honduras. Earlier in the day he and the orphanage mother went to the hospital in town for what was proclaimed as a broken arm. The doctor had taken an x-ray that exposed a total break in his arm. They had to return to the orphanage for some paperwork to move forward with the treatment. The Lord spoke to me to go and pray for him for a healing of the arm. I approached him, and the Lord said to ask him if he believed the Lord for his healing. So I asked him "do you have faith and believe the Lord for your healing?" he responded, "yes I completely believe." I asked him if I could lay hands on him for his healing and he was in absolute agreement. The Lord then spoke to me and had me take my cross off of my neck and present it to him as a gift of love. So I put the cross on his neck and commenced to pray and lay hands on him. I observed a fire in my hands, and he likewise felt the burning. That afternoon they returned to the hospital where they

Spiritual Pursuit

performed another x-ray, and no break could be visibly observed by X-ray. By the stripes of Jesus Christ, by the angelic intervention of God, he was miraculously healed and made whole.

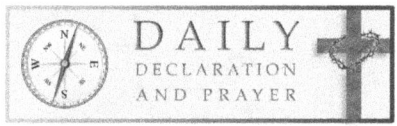

Father God, in Jesus' Name, I desire to approach your throne boldly and understand your voice uniquely in such a magnificent way that, Lord, I will indeed come to the deep place of the fullness of the mind of Christ Jesus, in Jesus Name, Amen!

DAY TWELVE

BE AWARE OF THE HOUR

But the Lord is faithful, who will establish you and
guard you from the evil one.
2 Thessalonians 3:3

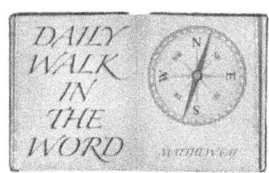

2 Thessalonians 2

Day Twelve

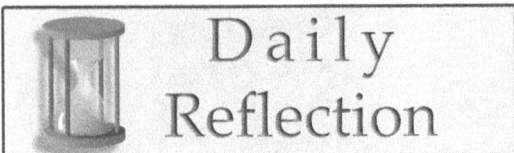
Daily Reflection

On these days we're living in, there are countless that are asleep, numb, and just slipping aside. These days, the enemy, Satan, and his demons are running around with many assignments on this earth in what would appear to be much power and influence. But the reality is, we must be conscious of one thing, Satan has no authority, except the authority and power we permit and empower him to have. The reality is God is summoning us out of this world. He wants to draw us away from the affairs of this world and bring us nearer into our walk with Him. That necessitates and requires a paradigm shift in thinking yes a renewing of the mind through His living word. We're called to possess the mind of Christ Jesus. That's a transformation in everything that we do yes our everyday life as we know it. If we don't walk away from the ways of this world, we will never develop and advance into His power and work in the Holy Spirit. Simply said if we do not renew our mind and surrender we will never access the fullness of His plan.

When we see Moses, we perceive him walking around for many years, trying to figure out more about wisdom,

Spiritual Pursuit

grasping the opportunity of actually coming to understand and comprehend how dependent he was on God and coming to find out that he must walk in the fullness of the power of God. The unfortunate reality was it took him forty years to figure these things out.

What does this have to do with us? I'm excited you asked! Countless times, we discovered that it takes many of us years to arrive to a place of really understanding the voice of God. We come to a place of discerning, to reach a place of being directed by God's leading and to truly know what the Lord is saying regarding our walk with Him, and His master plan.

Remember, we've been called in the representation of Christ Jesus. Remember, Jesus said 'Go and do what I did and do it greater.' That means we are commanded to be a light in the darkness, to be truth, to go and bring forth the same things that Jesus Christ did. We are ordered to walk in the abundance of power by the Holy Spirit. That means we must receive the fullness of the Holy Spirit and set no constraints on Him. We must not place God in a box. Any of these things will stop, limit or even hinder the supernatural movement and demonstration of The Holy Spirit of God. We aren't called to move in the Holy Spirit on certain days of the week or certain hours of the day, but rather, throughout our entire life. We are called to live a life in the Spirit, to obtain the fullness of what

Day Twelve

God has for each of us—great revelations from heaven, nuggets will be released into the place of our mind by the Spirit of God that will unlock doors not even possible by men.

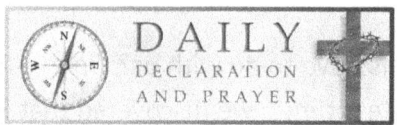

Father God, in Jesus' Name, I desire to come and hear the voice of God in such a great way that, Lord, I will truly come to the deep place of the fullness of the mind of Christ Jesus, in Jesus Name, Amen!

DAY THIRTEEN

DARE TO BELIEVE AND RECEIVE FROM GOD

Until now you have asked nothing in My name. Ask,
and you will receive, that your joy may be full.
John 16:24

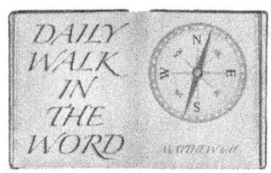

2 Chronicles 20:15-30

Day Thirteen

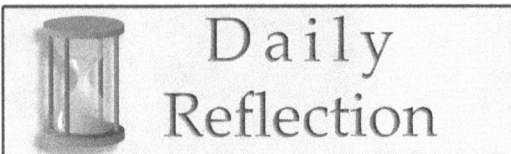
Daily Reflection

God has a definite plan for us, as He promised in Jeremiah 29:11 — a plan that is much greater and much broader than any of our thoughts. Many times, our thoughts can hinder the very things we ask God for. We need to strengthen our belief and trust the Lord. We must come to prayer with a unmovable understanding that Jesus Christ has such a strong understanding of the Father's power and is our only bridge to Him.

The certainty is, nothing is impossible for those who believe. And we are directed to ask, seek, and knock and the door will be opened. We must get rid of and dispose of all of our usual thinking habits. The fact is, they're hindering us from the blessings of the Lord. You ask why? I'm glad you asked. -Because God's desire is to transform us. He wants to make us a totally transformed person. He desires to make us in the likeness of Christ Jesus. His plan and purpose are to turn us into magnificent champions, but we've got to get past our natural thought process — yes, those things spinning around inside of our mind. We've got to get passed the constraints that we established in our mind.

Spiritual Pursuit

When we let go and start to trust God and believe God, we start to depend on His strength and that carries us to a Holy place of increase and understanding. What I'm saying directly is this, we need to come out of our ways of thinking, our limitations, and what we presume we can do, and proceed into the authority of the living God, trust Him and watch Him unfold great and mighty things. Today, this very day, as you read this entry, understand this: Today is an opportunity for a brand new beginning in your life, a brand new moment to step onward into a place, with God, you've never been before. A place of stepping into His truth, His promises, and His glory; ultimately, His abundant and overflowing blessings.

We must place fear underneath our feet and realize that we have a living God that created and arranged all things in order; that vocalized the very things of this earth unto creation. And understand this, we have no basis to fear anything on earth as we can accomplish all things through Jesus Christ who strengthens us, but we've got to believe, understand and acknowledge that God Almighty wants to deliver us up to fly on the wings of eagles and get to distinct altitudes every day.

Day Thirteen

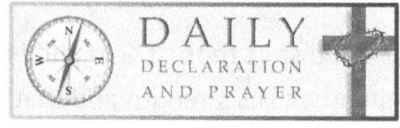

Father God, I embrace this day, Lord, to lay down my understanding and trust in you. I ask you Lord God to grow me, Lord, to bring me to greater elevations and believing, Lord, a greater understanding of your strength and power in my life. Lord, I abandon my ways to Yours and receive, God, Your abundant, overflowing blessings. I declare that I can do all things through Christ Jesus who strengthens me. And Lord, I ask you today with no fear, raise me Lord God, take me to new heights. I'm asking God for newer, larger things from this day forward, in Jesus' Name.

DAY FOURTEEN

THE AUTHORITY AND POWER OF THE BLOOD OF JESUS

> Through death He ... destroyed him who had the power of death, that is, the devil, and released those who through fear of death were all their lifetime subject to bondage.
> Hebrews 2:14-15

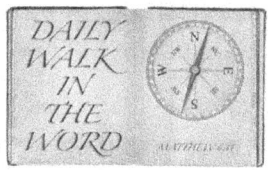

Hebrews 2:1-18

Day Fourteen

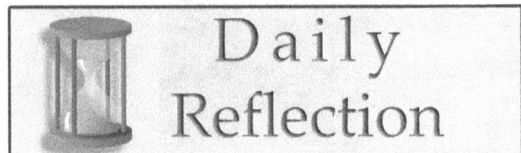

There's definitely an unlimited power in the blood of Jesus. The fact is, we're purchased through the very blood of Jesus. The precious, and living blood of Jesus makes our change, out of the darkness of this world and into the light of Christ, entirely possible. This amazing and highly blessed gift of salvation occurs through the blood of Jesus Christ and His death, burial, and resurrection ascending to the right hand of the Father and will entirely redeem us and deliver us from any and all power of Satan. The fact is: the Bible says we become joint heirs with Christ Jesus.

We see the Bible record in John 3:16 that God so loved the world that He sent His only begotten son. He sent Him with a plan, with a mission, and that was to rescue, redeem and save each of us. Through this plan, Jesus was manifested in the flesh. He was sent to destroy the very works of the enemy. Through Christ Jesus, we become champions/over-comers. The very power of the living and warm blood, through Christ Jesus, destroys the passions of this world for sin that have been residing in many of us through countless times by generational

Spiritual Pursuit

transfer from up to four generations back. These curses and tactics of the enemy are unusually long. As we begin to dwell in the Lord the curses and plans of the enemy are marvelously lifted away supernaturally. We can't make ourselves holy or righteous. It can only be fulfilled through Jesus Christ and His precious living blood. We need God to dwell in us just as He did Christ Jesus. The fact is, God can live in us through Christ Jesus by the Holy Spirit.

Jesus Christ chose to pay the cost at Calvary. He decided to die for each of us, resurrected three days later, walk this earth and ascend to Heaven. Because He was faithful, we were able to obtain the very sonship. When we look at the Bible, it says in Hebrews 5:8, though He was a Son, yet He mastered obedience by the things which He suffered. Many people think that Jesus Christ was a superstar and walked this earth in total favor. But no, the certainty is this: people slandered, denounced, and abused Him. That's right! They criticized Him in very abusive ways. They went at Him in very rude manners with great fury. In fact, they attempted to kill Him by tossing Him over a cliff, but by the grace of God, He went through the crowd and got out. After He had got away, He encountered a man in need of a miracle. This man was blind, and yes, Jesus healed him. Jesus Christ was in the world; however, He was not participating in the things of the world.

Day Fourteen

As we believe and have faith in Jesus Christ we truly see the power in the blood of Jesus; In the unfolding of His death, burial, resurrection, and in His ascension to the Fathers right hand in Heaven. The reality is when we accepted Jesus Christ and His fullness and surrendered and submitted to Him as seen in James 4:7-8, there's a extraordinary power that begins to work within us. Yes as our flesh starts to die and The Holy Spirit takes territory in our heart we begin to experience unusual power through the Holy Spirit. As this unfolds and we mature we come to a closer place of being moved, guided, and directed by the precious Holy Spirit into greater things of the Kingdom of God.

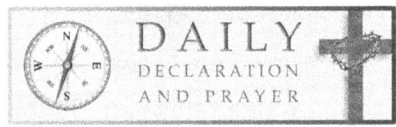

Father God, I declare now in Jesus' Name, I'm leaving a point of doubting and unbelief and entering a place of great belief and faith, God in You, the power of The Holy Spirit and Your Kingdom, in Jesus' Name.

DAY FIFTEEN

TRANSFORMED BY HIS LOVE

The sacrifices of God are a broken spirit, a broken and a contrite heart; these, O God, You will not despise.
Psalm 51:17

Psalm 51:1-17

Day Fifteen

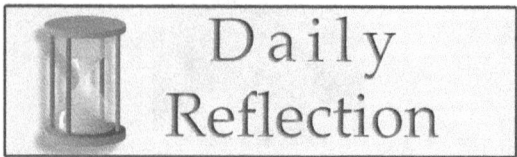
Daily Reflection

The abundance of the love and power of Christ Jesus brings us to know that there's something very distinctive about the love of the Lord, something so diverse that many don't understand it. It's different from a love scene or friendship or maybe a girlfriend or boyfriend. This is a different kind of love. In fact, in the Bible in 1 Peter 1:22, we see it referred to as a sincere love. That's right, a very different love from anything we've ever known! This love is one who will begin to lay our ways down as we're truly touched by His reliable, faithful and genuine love as he begins to move upon our life. In Romans 5:8, the Bible says that he loved you when you were yet a sinner. And the reality is, He doesn't just love us for anything. It's a relationship. He desires our love in return. His love is powerful, great and mighty. It's a love that can endure while people are projecting accusations, persecutions and slanderous statements towards you. It's a love that's brought forth by the Holy Spirit—the very love that transforms us from one person into a completely transformed one.

Spiritual Pursuit

Everything about us shifts when we're touched by His love through the Holy Spirit because there is nothing in this world like Him. In fact, even your natural bodies will begin to go through change. He will start to strengthen you and produce right transformation into your life. He is the God that loves us with a genuine love, the God that loves the sinner, the God that's full of mercy. He is the God that loves the helpless and God overflowing in mercy and grace. When we look at Exodus chapter 3, we see Him referred to as the God of Jacob. So no matter how faraway you've wondered, as God did with Jacob, God will restore you back to the same place, no matter how far away from the course you have wondered. It's time to let everything go and let God. Many times, we presume that we're perfect, that we are correct, that we had the right, but truthfully, it took one touch from God for Jacob, just one touch, and Jacob discovered that he had nothing good in him. As God met Jacob, He wants to meet each of us in our situation of suffering, in our tears, in our broken hearts, and in our sorrow. These valleys are some of the closest places where God comes to meet us and show us His love.

Day Fifteen

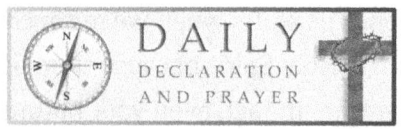

Father God, in Jesus' Name, engage me in my brokenness, in my tears, in my hurts and pains. I lay it down today, and I declare I am letting go and letting God. Engage me as you did Jacob, Lord. Meet me, God, and return me to where I need to be. In Jesus' Name!

DAY SIXTEEN

LIBERATION FROM FEAR

There is no fear in love; but perfect love casts out fear.
1 John 4:18

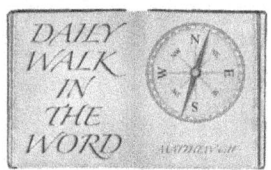

1 John 4:7-21

Day Sixteen

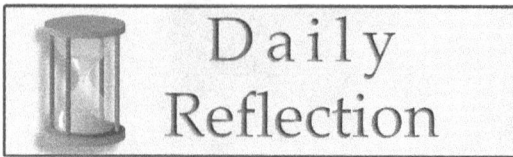
Daily Reflection

It's necessary that we nevermore fear anything. You say anything? That's right! Nothing at all! The Bible tells there is no fear in love, but in fact, perfect love casts out all fear. So, there are two things that we can look at concerning this fear—one is a place of giving in to fear, or the other is a place of living on our faith. And yes, that's where we need to be. Why? Well, one of these belongs to the enemy. That's right—belongs to the devil. But the other—that's when we endure and stand on our faith—this is of God. That is where we need to be.

When we stand on God's truth, when we truly believe in God, there's no place for fear to exist. Looking at 1 John 4:18, it says, there is no fear in love, but perfect love casts out all fear. Who is love? That's exactly right—the Lord Jesus Christ. The enemy came to steal, kill, and destroy. He always tries to bind us up. You know he uses the very rope we give him, and that's when he bind us. He tries to put us in a place of bondage, but when we stand firmly on the truth of the Lord Jesus Christ, we seat ourselves in place of His perfect love. And we know as

Spiritual Pursuit

the Bible says, perfect love casts out every bit of fear—all of it!

So anything that tries to come and make you frightened, bring anxiety, horror or terror, or bind you, don't open into that. Never allow it because remember, with the enemy, we have to allow him to have authority. He doesn't have authority over us. The Bible says in Romans 8:31 that if God is for us, who can be against us. That's right—no one at all!

We've talked before in this journal about the importance of the Holy Spirit filling us, saturating our hearts, filling our body, completely filling us. This place of coming into complete belief is no different. With the Holy Spirit, we come into that full place of freedom.

I once heard we can't live on a former anointing. That means we can't live on something that happened yesterday or two weeks ago, two years ago or however long behind us. We live today, and the Holy Spirit daily fills our hearts with love, truth, and peace. We never go backward and depend on something in the past, any person, place or thing, but exclusively on the Holy Spirit everyday.

Remember, the Holy Spirit doesn't want to be seen. He wants Jesus Christ to be recognized, and Jesus Christ

Day Sixteen

says, if you've seen Him, you've seen the Father. See the order there? That's in order of love because it all started with the Father. For God so loved the world, He gave His only begotten Son (John 3:16). That's right! So, as we're living every day with the Holy Spirit, we know one thing: God Almighty is going to pour out His anointing upon us, pour out his blessings upon us, and pour his treasures upon us like we've never seen before. There's nothing more that God wants than to saturate us with the fullness of His love.

So many times, we have slipped and fallen short of God's glory and grace and so many times, it's because we have pushed the Holy Spirit away when He's attempted to come and guide us in the right direction. It's important to repent for those times and invite Him back. It's vital that we allow the precious Holy Spirit to bring forth a great light that overtakes us and brings us an abundance of joy, peace, and hope because as we're filled like this, there is no darkness that will be upon us.

Today I encourage you, grab your freedom in the Lord Jesus Christ and the Holy Spirit and push away all fear. Take the Lord's truth now from His Word and every day consume it, and read it. Let this truth be the authentic light for your path. And remember this very thing, that it's Jesus Christ expired on the cross for each of us, and was buried, arose again, and ascended to the right hand

Spiritual Pursuit

of the Father. His blood shed, and the very blood that shed is the very blood that is living and cleanses us from all sin. We find that in 1 John 1:7.

Today, rest in His peace. Know that his peace is for you. Take a moment, get before Him, repent of all sins, known and unknown in your life, and receive and reside in the fullness of His peace today. If you're carrying anything in your heart toward anyone, forgive, let go and let God. Ask the Lord to bring the healing, peace, and joy that only He can bring into your heart. Because remember, in 1 Samuel 16:7, God looks at the inward heart, but the man looks at the outward appearance. Make it a point today as you are living in liberation from fear to live in a life forgiving others daily, to live a life of complete repentance, and to live a life that your heart is set upon the Lord. A life of obedience and sacrifice to the Lord. Doing these things will bring harmony in your life aligned with the Lord God Almighty.

Day Sixteen

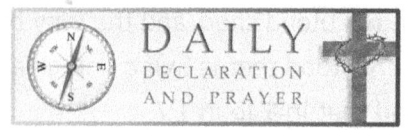

Father God, in the Name of Jesus, now Lord, I just want to come and place everything down at your feet. Today, I forgive everyone and today, Lord, I accept and receive full forgiveness. Today, I repent for each sin, known and unknown in my life and ask you to forgive me. I accept Lord God, the fullness of your freedom from many and all fear the enemy has tried to come and bring to my life. I refuse to fear and I receive life in the Lord Jesus Christ today. In Jesus Name, Amen!

DAY SEVENTEEN

FAITH-NOT SOULISH FEELINGS

He who believes in the Son of God has the witness in himself.
1 John 5:10

1 John 5:6-17

Day Seventeen

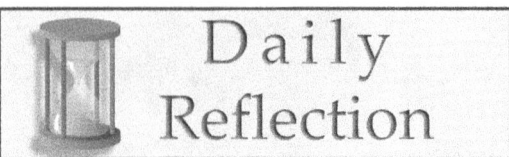
Daily Reflection

So many times in ministry and my everyday walk, I find people walking in a really deceived state. Many times, I've seen people that have experienced the loss of businesses, homes, marriages, and family members, to name just a few. And the foremost reason they've had these losses is they were operating out of a soulish realm, going off of feelings. I hear people so many times, 'I feel this' or 'I feel that' but the truth is, feelings are not proceeding from the Lord Jesus Christ, aren't coming by way of the Holy Spirit for the answer / the direction.

So, we move out of our faith, not feelings. Remember, we are striving always to be God-pleasers. We are sons and daughters of the living God. Not man-pleasers! Our heart should always be set to excellence and obedience to Him. We are commanded to be in this world but not of this world. God is ready to flow through you in a very supernatural way by His Holy Spirit. Yes, He wants to bring you from the natural to the supernatural. As we walk deeper in the Spirit, we must put to death many things in our 'soulish' nature—that is, our natural life. Let us daily be guided by the Spirit of God, let us dispossess

Spiritual Pursuit

our 'soulish' nature and let us dive into a great place of belief. Remember the Bible informs us, most assuredly, I say to you, he who believes in me has everlasting life. I am the bread of life— John 6:47-48. Remember, we cannot live off of the bread of this world, but the bread He is speaking of here, the bread of life, is that bread of the Word of God, the living God.

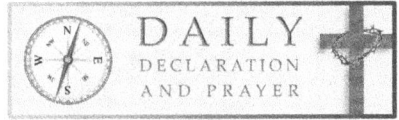

Heavenly Father, everything I require is in you. Today, I lay down a place of working out of feelings and step forth into operating out of faith. I welcome you Holy Spirit and acknowledge you and respond, have your way. Lead me to a glorious life in the Spirit, greater peace, love, and your abundant outpouring of what you've set before me. Today, I open my belief and faith to receive what you provide by your spirit, and the truth and the very bread of life— that is, the life of your Word.

DAY EIGHTEEN

YOU ARE AN EPISTLE OF CHRIST

You are an epistle of Christ.
2 Corinthians 3:3

Colossians 3:16 – 4:6

Day Eighteen

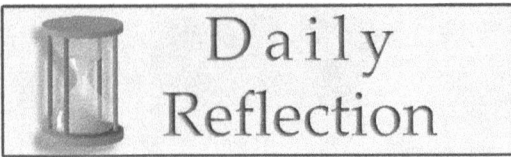
Daily Reflection

No matter where we stay while we're on this earth—in what city, town, or country—there are rules put in place by men to keep order, to maintain the peace. We refer to the these as the laws of the land, but one thing we know is this-this is not our home. We're here temporarily according to the Bible in Philippians 3:20. The Bible says our citizenship is in heaven. As we look around in our day to day life, whether it's at work, at school, on a bus or wherever you may venture through your day, you will see this planet filled with broken people, broken hearts, broken dreams—so many broken pieces. When we surrender to Jesus Christ and give our lives to Him and submit to His ways, we become a redeemed people in the Lord, and we are transformed for His glory.

In this journey, we talk a lot about being saturated with the Holy Spirit and being guided by the Holy Spirit. This is another important reason why we need to be influenced by the Holy Spirit—it's that, we live in the Spirit and not in the law. We allow the precious Holy Spirit to influence, guide and direct our steps and paths of righteousness for God's glory. Many times, the Holy

Spiritual Pursuit

Spirit will use us on this earth to reach the broken people as a vessel of honor. He will utilize us to speak on His behalf. The only way to reliably be a mouthpiece for God is to be abandoned, submitted and obedient. In a sense, we are hosting Him and need to take great care not to quench His presence. Allowing the precious Holy Spirit to speak through us is the perfect will of God.

The Bible says in 2 Corinthians 3:17, Now the Lord is the Spirit: and where the Spirit of the Lord is, there is liberty. So the very things the Holy Spirit will speak through us brings healing, restoration and the freeing of people, not to mention that He desires to use you as a mouthpiece in the process. He wants to divinely use each of us for His glory and His purposes. Many times, He may have you share your personal testimony. In the book of Revelation we read that by the blood of the lamb and word of our testimony, the enemy is overtaken. The significant thing here again is that the Spirit influences us. We don't become too wordy when we speak but surrendered in our speaking to The Holy Spirit. We speak what He would have us to speak. Again, this is for people's freedom and God's glory. It's not something you sit down and prepare for or write out ahead of time per se. We come forth with a broken heart and a contrite spirit, and we yield ourselves to the Holy Spirit and say 'have your way' and let him do just that.

Day Eighteen

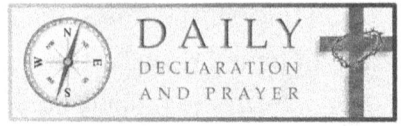

Father God, in Jesus' Name, I submit my will and my ways to you and invite you to have your way. Speak through me, use me, as I yield to you with a broken heart a contrite Spirit for your glory, in Jesus' Name.

DAY NINETEEN

PEACE AND HOPE

May the God of hope fill you with all joy and peace in
believing, that you may abound in hope by the power
of the Holy Spirit.
Romans 15:13

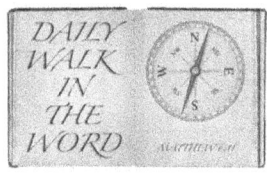

Ephesians 1:2 – 21

Day Nineteen

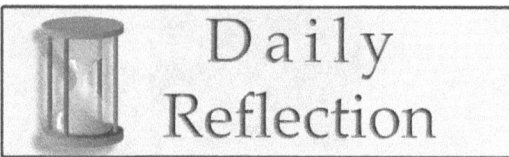
Daily Reflection

Living a surrendered and laid-down-life before the Lord is essential. As we live a sanctified life in the Holy Spirit, we come to an amazing deep place of true rest in Him- an actual place of total peace and relaxation. The more we press into this place and rest in Him, we'll begin to receive revelation through the Holy Spirit. Yes, we begin to be taken into heavenly places and heavenly realms. You say, how is that possible? I'm glad you asked. The Holy Spirit comes, and He talks with us. He desires a relationship and, therefore, He comes Himself and speaks to us. As He comes and converses, He brings revelation. We begin to walk in and receive such a deep place of His peace. And as we look at the Word of God, we see that peace in Philippians 4:7 – a peace which surpasses all understanding.

His passion is a relationship with us. He has such an extraordinary love for each of us. He desires our cup to run over. Yep, He sure does! Psalm 23:5, it says how the Holy Spirit fills our cups full and running over. In Nehemiah 8:10, we see, He also wants to bring tremendous joy to us. "The joy of the Lord is your

Spiritual Pursuit

strength." Let us never forget; He is our peace and hope. And again, we encounter the fullness of Him through the Holy Spirit and the Living Word of God.

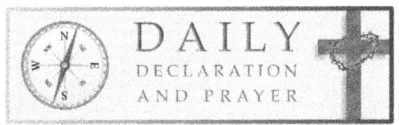

Father God, in Jesus Name, I receive the fullness of your peace and hope. Holy Spirit, cause my cup to run over. And I declare that the joy of the Lord is my strength. I declare that your peace and hope fill my life every day and every way, in Jesus Name.

DAY TWENTY

GOD IS WITH YOU

No temptation has overtaken you except such as is common to man; but God is faithful, who will not allow you to be tempted beyond what you are able, but with the temptation will also make the way of escape, that you may be able to bear it.
1 Corinthians 10:13

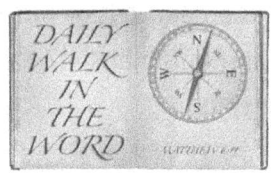

Romans 8:31-39

Day Twenty

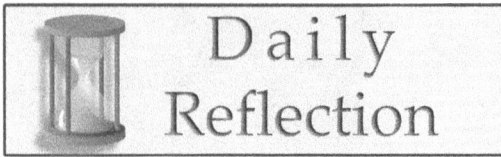
Daily Reflection

Living a surrendered, obedient and laid-down-life before the Lord is essential. As we live a sanctified life in the Holy Spirit, we come to an amazing deep place of true rest in Him- an actual place of total peace and relaxation. The more we press into this place and rest in Him, we'll begin to receive revelation through the Holy Spirit. Yes, we begin to be taken into heavenly places and heavenly realms.

You say, how is that possible? I'm glad you asked. The Holy Spirit comes, and He talks with us. He desires a relationship and, therefore, He comes Himself and speaks to us. As He comes and converses, He brings revelation. We begin to walk in and receive such a deep place of His peace. And as we look at the Word of God, we see that peace in Philippians 4:7 — a peace which surpasses all understanding.

His passion is a relationship with us. He has such an extraordinary love for each of us. He desires our cup to run over. Yep, He sure does! Psalm 23:5, it says how the Holy Spirit fills our cups full and running over. In

Spiritual Pursuit

Nehemiah 8:10, we see, He also wants to bring tremendous joy to us. "The joy of the Lord is your strength." Let us never forget; He is our peace and hope. And again, we encounter the fullness of Him through the Holy Spirit and the Living Word of God.

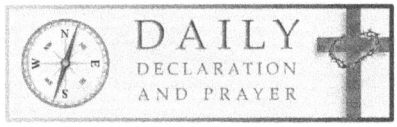

Father God, in Jesus' Name, I thank you for never leaving me nor forsaking me. I thank you that you are my ever present help in time of need. And I thank you that I trust you, Lord. I walk in the trials and tribulations, God, that I can prove myself faithful and grow to greater heights in your Kingdom, in Jesus' Name.

DAY TWENTY-ONE

EXPERIENCE HIS JOY

Count it all joy when you fall into various trials.
James 1:2

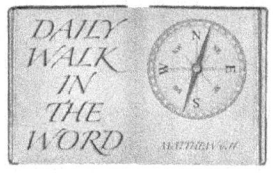

1 Peter 5:5-11

Day Twenty-One

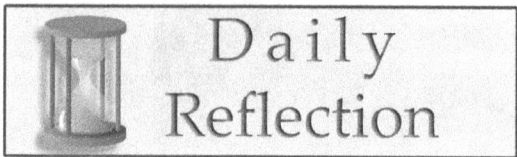
Daily Reflection

I believe that we have passed through a day or time when trials have come up, and we've sunk into immense sadness. But today, take and cast that depression and doubt outside. Place it beneath your feet. Today, cry out to the Lord Jesus Christ because He's listening. Pride will rob you and make you fall. Just cry out and expose every feeling and doubt you have. Hold nothing back and tell Him everything. He's all-knowing. The reality is, He secures every tear that we shed in a bottle of our tears.

When we look at Psalm 30:5, we know that sorrow may come at night, but joy comes in the morning. So many times, we never look upward and shout out to God, and that's the exact thing we need do. God is listening to us. He's a God of love and relationship. In John 11:41, Jesus says, "Father, I thank you that you have heard me." Look at that—that you have heard me. God is listening to us.

He desires this relationship with us. He seeks to touch us and bring a new peace into our condition. He seeks to bring the supernatural into our natural. He wants to hold nothing back as He's a good Father. Some of you are

Spiritual Pursuit

probably responding right now, "I just can't believe that." But it's the truth. In James 1:5, "God gives to all liberally and without reproach."

As we read about in this journal so many times concerning surrendering to the Spirit and trusting the Lord, today, I urge you, lay it all down. Believe Him. Give doubt no place because He wants to pour out on you like never before. Those thoughts that say, "I've done so much. I've gone too far. I passed the point of no return" No! In Jesus' Name, our God is a merciful and loving God —a God that fulfills all of our needs; a God that's waiting for the real knock on the door, so He can open it and pour out His abundance upon us and our circumstances. He's not human; He's God! And He is well able and prepared to provide our every requirement.

He wants to satisfy every aspect of our lives with His abundance. Let us go today, as we see in 1 Peter 5:7, and bring all of our cares upon Him for He cares for us. Remember this—God will never leave us nor forsake us. He loves us, and He wants to help us. Today, lay it all down before Him. Call out and experience the fullness of His joy.

Day Twenty-One

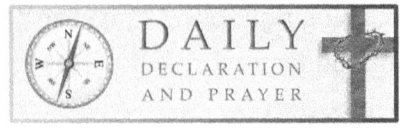

Father God, in Jesus' Name, I know that when I enter trials and tribulations, I'm not alone. You said you'll never leave me nor forsake me. I know when I'm at my lowest and it looks like you're nowhere around, you're right there with me closer than my own breath. I thank you Lord God Almighty that your joy is available now and I receive it! I lay it all down before you Lord and open up to receive the fullness of your joy, in Jesus' Name.

DAY TWENTY-TWO

SONSHIP

Behold what manner of love the Father has bestowed
on us, that we should be called children of God!
1 John 3:1

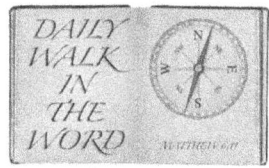

John 1:1-13

Day Twenty-Two

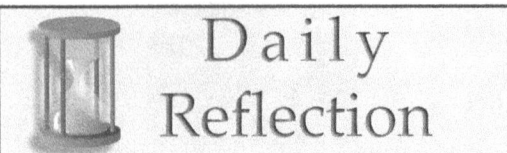
Daily Reflection

God is great in all things. The things He does for us are larger than life. The reality is, the nearer we walk to Him, the more wonderful our walk is in His presence. We go back and look at John 17:15-16, and it says, "I do not pray that you should take them out of the world. They are not of the world." We must understand that fully. Let's pause for a second and grasp that. This is a tremendous Revelation that we need to know. He says do not pray that you should take them out of the world— in other words, that's us—because they are not of the world. In other words, we are visitors here on a mission. We are God's ambassadors, His children on assignment in this place called earth.

The fact is 1 John 3:2 says, "Beloved, now we are children of God." God Almighty has a plan and a purpose for each of our lives. But to comprehend that, we've got to delve into His Scripture, the truth, and advance very sincerely in the Holy Spirit. These words of the Bible are merely words unless all of us, genuine believers, have the absolute confidence that as we believe and walk in His truth, we dwell in Him. Yes, we abide in His truth.

Spiritual Pursuit

I listen to so many people going around and quoting the Bible. But many times, they almost seem like a parrot, where they're just quoting the Bible, yet the parrot is still locked in the cage. We've been invited to a place of walking in victory, not to be stuck in a cage. And we've got to recognize that the spirit of God is within us and He is living. 1 John 4:4 says, He who is in us is greater than he who is in the world. What does this mean? There's nothing too difficult or troublesome for Him. There's no enemy greater than Him. There's no darkness greater than Him. He is all-powerful and greater than everything, and He is in us. We must arrive to the understanding of how high and mighty the Holy Spirit is because He's greater than every difficulty or hindrance.

Every measure of darkness that exists in this world will never be greater, Holy Spirit is powerful, and yes, He is within us! Here's where we cross the bridge—we must get to a place of knowing His Word deeply in our heart. Yes, we need the knowledge, but we can't just go around quoting the Word. We need the abundance in our heart. Why? His Word is full of promises, and we need to possess those promises in our heart. God never called us to be just common people. There are many, many, many average people in this world, and He never charged us to be just regular people. He called us to be extraordinary people to stand out. Regular people do not arrive at a

Day Twenty-Two

point of merit with God. The truth is, God called us as ambassadors. He called us to be extraordinary. He called us to stand out for His glory. That's correct—to magnify Him. This is why we need to press-in to His Word / His Truth, to get to such a mysterious place in His Holy Spirit that God would come in and take us beyond like never before moving us in such profound power.

We are to be so full with Jesus that we're overflowing. Remember, we've been summoned to be in the likeness of Christ Jesus and in the Bible. He ordered us to go and do what He did and greater. Before the foundations of the world, He set a plan forth for each of us, a divine plan. So many people have moved in this world in their flesh and a place of failing and instability for so long, but God has not called us to weakness.

He's called us to a place of surrender and obedience, to a place of moving and burning in the Holy Spirit's power. Yes, we pass through trials and tribulations. Praise the Lord! But Jesus went through even greater trials. Hebrews 4:15 says, He was in all points tempted as we are, yet without sin. What's the purpose behind this? To be able to go through these things that we can encourage, assist, and support others who are oppressed in the same way.

Spiritual Pursuit

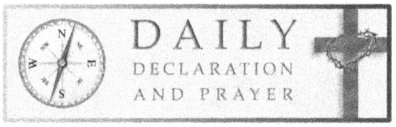

Father God, in Jesus' Name, I lay down my knowledge, opinion, perception and my weakness of this world before you. And thank you that you didn't ask me to be ordinary or regular, but extraordinary. I embrace this now and say, have your way. I acknowledge myself as a child of the Most High God. I thank you for He that is in me because He is greater than he who is in the world. Have your way in my life, Lord, in Jesus' Name, Amen!

DAY TWENTY-THREE

ALIVE TO GOD

Now if we died with Christ, we believe that we shall also live with Him.
Romans 6:8

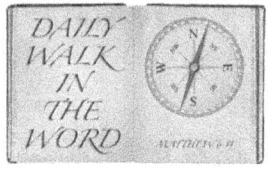

Romans 6

Day Twenty-Three

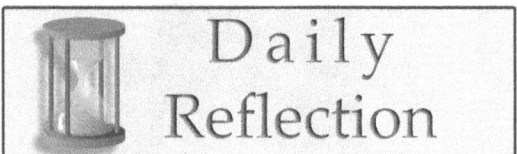
Daily Reflection

In the Word of God, we examine the Apostle Paul, and he couldn't have communion with flesh and blood. There was no way. Why? It would not allow him to go forward in the Lord's plan. When we look at Jesus in His time on this earth, we even see Jesus' view on this in Matthew 12:48-50, "Who is my mother and who are my brothers?" And He stretched out his hands towards his disciples and said, "Here are my mom and my brothers! For whoever does the will of my Father in heaven is my brother and sister and mother."

Jesus had no interest in just flesh and blood. God brought Jesus Christ to this world for an important purpose. The fact is, He came to this world as a Seed, and that seed was life for each of us. So, you're looking at the Scripture here, and you see that the faithful believer was his mother. You comprehend the very servant of God was His brother. And the follower of Christ himself was his sister. Wow!

Ultimately, Jesus is beckoning us to die to our self, to die to our flesh, and to come to a new life to be alive in God

Spiritual Pursuit

Almighty. Yes, praise the Lord! Jesus had to endure many sufferings while on this earth as a part of being that Seed of Life. You see Him in his human nature in Matthew 26:39, crying out, "If it is possible, let this cup pass from me." A little later, he goes on to say in verse 39, "Nevertheless, not as I will but as you will." A little bit further, in the book of John 12:27, He says, "But for this purpose, I came to this hour." As you recall, we said as He came as the Seed of Life. He gave us life, but in that, the very aspect of his human place here had to come to a conclusion. There were no more choices. And that's when He proceeded to face the cross at Calvary.

When we can see this picture of what Jesus went through, recognize and accept it, the Holy Spirit can bring us to a place where we will desire to deny ourselves for the sake of Christ dying on that cross that we would live. That means we must die to our flesh. That means all the natural things that attract and pull at us need to die and our focus needs to be affixed on the spiritual things of heaven—that is, through the Word of God and by His Spirit.

God granted us free will, and by that very free will, we need to allow Him to come in and have command of our life. As we do that, He will take us to greater extraordinary places in Him, through deeper graces than we've ever seen before. We need to establish our eyes on

Day Twenty-Three

the matters of the Kingdom and not on the opinions of the world. The real treasures are in Jesus Christ. The real treasures come by faith and not by sight.

We have been commanded as believers to bear fruit unto the Lord. -Romans 7:4. My brothers and sisters, I implore you today to look through the lens of the Lord God Almighty and see how very wealthy you are in the Kingdom and not by the measurement of this world.

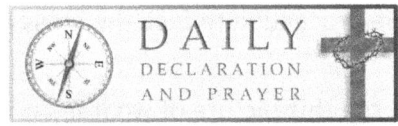

Father God, in Jesus' Name, I thank you Lord that my human nature no longer rules and reigns over my life. I submit God to the Holy Spirit. I become to see the truths, Oh God, as I deny myself and come to a greater place in Thee. Lord, I surrender my life and I walk to you this day. in Jesus' Name, Amen!

DAY TWENTY-FOUR

WHAT DOES IT MEAN TO BELIEVE?

And the evil spirit answered and said, "Jesus I know, and Paul I know; but who are you?"
Acts 19:15

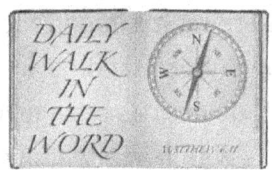

Acts 19:11-20

Day Twenty-Four

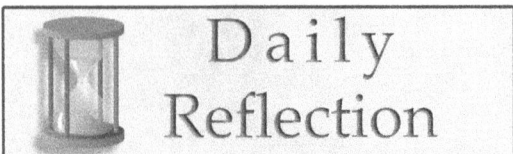
Daily Reflection

I ask you this question today—what is belief? Do you know? I think many times; people have a very widespread answer on things. But to believe is an vital part of your walk with the Lord.

A huge part of belief is to have an adequate understanding of what you believe in, not just a general opinion. At this point, you're probably wondering— Richard, what exactly are you saying? Well, let me put it like this. So many people in the world today just believe in the word, but they don't have actual experience or understanding of His fullness. They don't understand the nature of Jesus Christ. They don't understand the commission of Jesus Christ, nor do they understand the vision of Jesus Christ. But it's important that we truly have knowledge and understanding so we can honestly believe because all power has been given unto Him and greater is He who is within you than he who is in the world (1 John 4:4).

So many times, in our Christian walk, we just want to be spick-and-span overnight. You know, fully washed and

Spiritual Pursuit

polished up, fully delivered. But that's not how it works. With that thought process, so many people ran around shouting out the name of Jesus toward these demons, thinking there is power in the name only when there is power is in the knowledge, belief and knowing what He's done.

Understanding His vision and His mission, and certainly, to know His full nature and we get that in the Word of God and the knowledge, facts, and belief we get from the Word of God, not just knowing only the name of Jesus. The sons of Sceva went around using the name of Jesus and the demons laughed. We must understand this; the real power comes by way of the Holy Spirit where we get a big revelation of the abundance of Christ and His glory. It's understanding in our heart that all authority has been given to Jesus Christ.

It's in the understanding of the knowledge of Jesus Christ, His mission, and through faith that we have in Him. The demons have no option but to surrender, come out and flee and the sons of Sceva went forth just using the name of Jesus with no strong understanding, revelation or knowledge of Him. The demons told him, "Jesus I know and Paul I know..." Effectively, they're stating, "You're nothing but a man. You have no power, no authority."

Day Twenty-Four

It's crucial that we come to know Jesus Christ and His fullness through His Word by the precious Holy Spirit. We must come to know Him that we are overflowing with His presence, with the knowledge of Him, with his vision and mission. Know one thing—Jesus Christ is King over all demons and all darkness. And every evil power is subject to Jesus Christ who is manifested in us by the Holy Spirit. Yes, all the demons, devils, and darkness know Jesus Christ. We have to die to ourselves that He can indeed become greater. We have to become least. We must abandon our lives and ourselves to Him in every way every day that He can come in and manifest in our lives because when this happens, there's no effort on our part to see authority and the power of Jesus manifesting through the Holy Spirit that the devils are running from.

We must surrender our lives to Him and come to a place of greater holiness. All powers of darkness know this. They truly know who Jesus Christ is. As the word of God says, "Jesus I know and Paul I know, but who are you?" Alone, the devils are not afraid of you or me. They tremble and run from Jesus Christ and the Holy Spirit who is in us greater than he who is in the world. The Holy Spirit has come into us to be the judge of this world of sin and unbelief. In John 16:7-11, the Word of God says this, "Nevertheless, I tell you the truth, it is expedient for you that I go away, for if I go not away, the

Spiritual Pursuit

Comforter will not come unto you. But if I depart, I will send Him unto you. When He has come, He will reprove the world of sin and of righteousness and of judgment— of sin, because they believe not on me; of righteousness, because I go to my Father and ye see me no more; of judgment because the prince of this world is judged." We want a seal of approval from God, knowing that Jesus knows us, but also knowing that the devil knows us and He who is in us.

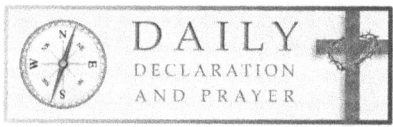

Father God, in Jesus' Name, I thank you for greater belief in my life, Lord. I yield and surrender that I would come to have the stamp of approval from you, Jesus, that you would know me, but the devil would clearly know me as well, for He who is in me is greater than he who is in the world. Thank you for a greater place of holiness in my life, so that everything that is not like you Jesus has to depart today, in Jesus' Name.

DAY TWENTY-FIVE

GOD IS NEAR

"Behold, the virgin shall be with child, and bear a Son, and they shall call His name Immanuel," which is translated, "God with us."
Matthew 1:23

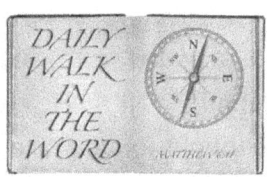

Matthew 1:18-25; Philippians 2:5-11

Day Twenty-Five

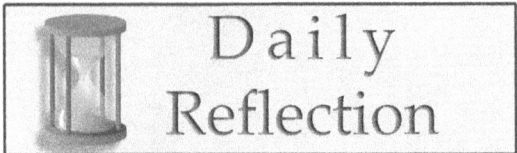
Daily Reflection

In life, there are many truths and many realities. Many times, we choose not to accept the truth of those realities, but one of those facts is having salvation in the Lord Jesus Christ. It is a vital truth and reality. People today are roaming around on antidepressive medications and all these different medicines. Some prefer to self-medicate with alcohol, drugs, sex, and many other devices that aren't of God. In actuality, it's the enemy's tools, weapons, and methods to bind and render many people helpless, but the certainty is when we are truly safe, and we acknowledge that we possess the peace of God in our lives. Freedom fully comes through Jesus Christ and no other source or place.

He spoke, you shall know the truth, and the truth shall make you free in John 8:32 NKJV. He also tells us, hold your peace and I will fight for you take a look at Exodus 14:14. Numerous times I have witnessed Satan come along and displace and separate people from God's perfect plan—some of the most significant people—because they're not advancing in the wisdom and knowledge of God, growing and being guided by the

Spiritual Pursuit

Holy Spirit of God. These people are delayed and restrained under a spirit of deception. They're deceived by believing and accepting the lies of the enemy. Remember, Jesus said in Luke 19:10, "I have come to save those who are lost." And we find Jesus in the Word of God and the Great Comforter he sent—the Holy Spirit. So many are discouraged, confused, scared, and depressed today and feel like so many things they've done disqualify them, have brought them to a conclusion, or that it's just 'game over.' But that's far away from the truth. When the devil's nearest, God's even nearer. The reality is He's closer to you than your breath. When you're wandering around feeling disappointed, broken or defeated, God is there cheering you on and encouraging you to overcome and succeed. Call out to Him just ask, seek and knock the door will be opened. Remember something— His mercy and His grace are more than sufficient.

We need to dig into the knowledge of God and open to The Holy Spirit to breathe upon you and be overtaken by the Holy Spirit of God. He's arrived to deliver and redeem us. We need to recognize one thing, His redemption is real, and He is perfect, and He's arrived to rescue and restore us. So today, stop being your harshest critic. Quit judging yourself. Run from the devil. James 4:7 says, Submit yourselves therefore to God. Resist the devil, and he will flee from you. It goes on in verse 8 to say, Draw

Day Twenty-Five

nigh to God, and He will draw nigh to you. Cleanse your hands, ye sinners; and purify your hearts, ye double-minded. Verse 9, Be afflicted, and mourn, and weep: let your laughter be turned to mourning and your joy to heaviness. Verse 10, Humble yourselves in the sight of the Lord, and he shall lift you up. The thing we must realize from that is to submit. We've got to surrender ourselves to God's plan. God is near us, and he wants to deliver and restore us today. He wants to guide us out of these earthly places into a higher place in His Spirit with great power and authority. Allow today be the day to enter completely in!

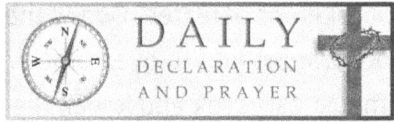

Father God, in Jesus' Name, I thank you, Lord, that Jesus chose to reach out of heaven into this earth for me. Lord, I thank you for your mercy and grace and today, I want your redemption. I acknowledge that you are nearer to me than ever before I choose to draw nigh to you, God and submit to you and I ask you to draw nigh to me. In Jesus' Name, Amen!

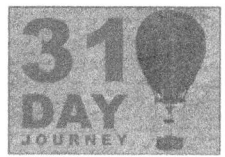

DAY TWENTY-SIX

WHAT IS YOUR MOTIVE?

You ask and do not receive, because you ask amiss,
that you may spend it on your pleasures.
James 4:3

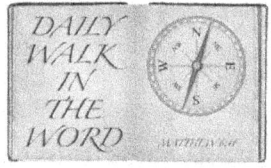

Ephesians 1:3-14

Day Twenty-Six

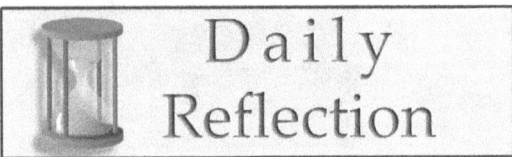
Daily Reflection

In the Bible, we're shown to ask, seek, and knock and the door will be answered. You will seek, and you will encounter the Lord. Many times, we seek this on the drive-through plan—you know, the microwave method: 'We want it immediately! We don't want to have to put the time in or wait.' But that is not how the Kingdom advances. The actuality is this; God says in Matthew 7:8, "Everyone who asks, receives." So what are you seeking God for? What are you asking Him for today? What have you been asking Him for in the past? What's the motivation behind your asking and wanting?

In the Kingdom of God, there are gifts, and we require those gifts of The Holy Spirit to serve in the Kingdom and attain ground. You understand, to advance! Let us seek out the Kingdom of God and ask Him to reveal to each of us what gifts He wants us to have. Since the reality is, you will never be happy, content, or satisfied until you're walking in His path. Walking in His abundance, ultimately receiving these gifts and operating in them. The truth is, my brothers and sisters, many times we imagine we're special or have some

Spiritual Pursuit

control or power, but the fact check arrives now. We can do nothing by ourselves, but we can do all everything through Christ Jesus who strengthens us. God Almighty has taken off the past, garments that we had as a natural man and placed brand-new garments on us as we come to Him—garments of power. Why? -Because these very garments are God and His shelter and cover, and He is the highest and greatest power. When we take on this new power, which is His hand/His covering upon us, we go forth in His abundance and His strength by His Holy Spirit. And that is when we start to see the actions of the church of Acts unfold. That's right! See the things that took place in the days of the earliest disciples unfolding in our very lives. We require more of the Holy Spirit, not just a touch from the Holy Spirit here and there, but to walk in the fullness and overflow of the Spirit of God. We have got to desire and require Him to abide in us. We need to absolutely surrender to the Spirit and desire to be guided by him, but we must be ready to deny ourselves, the things we crave in this world and surrender to his abundance and his direction, as we do that, God will cause the rain to pour out his revelation in such manner. It's difficult to explain. When this happens, there is genuinely a baptism in the Holy Spirit that takes place and, indeed a fullness of his Spirit flowing in our lives. This is what places a smile on the face of God and causes Him to be satisfied and nothing less. He only desires the greatest for His children. And today, I

Day Twenty-Six

question you, are you ready to surrender your life and your ways that He can fill you to the fullness and utilize you in a way he did with the original disciples in the book of Acts? Miracles, Signs, and Wonders... The sick healed, dead raised, and devils cast out of people? This awaits you!

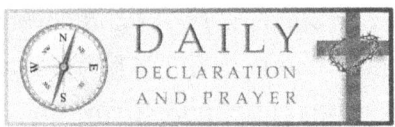

Father God, in Jesus' Name, you said in your Word that everyone who asks, receives; and everyone who seeks, finds; and to knock and the door will be opened. So today, I'm knocking, seeking, and asking to receive. I can't do anything on my own God, and I acknowledge that before you. I ask you to come and clothe me, Lord God put a new garment on me and bring me closer to you. Lord, I'm willing to deny my flesh, to deny myself to things of this world and surrender to your plan for my life. I hunger and thirst for a deeper relationship and greater revelation of your Truth to be flowing over me in the fullness of your precious Holy Spirit. Come today, in Jesus' Name, Amen!

DAY TWENTY-SEVEN

PRAYING IN THE SPIRIT

I will pray with the spirit, and I will also pray with the understanding.
1 Corinthians 14:15

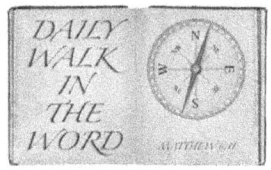

Hebrews 7:11-28

Day Twenty-Seven

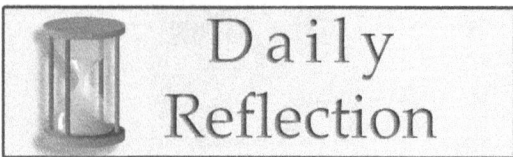
Daily Reflection

I want to share an important testimony with you regarding praying in the Spirit. This choice either brings an increase in your spiritual life or without a spiritual decline. Many people walk this world today without a necessary understanding of the power of praying in the Spirit. The fact is, there is tremendous power in speaking in the unknown tongue of the Holy Spirit. As I give this testimony, my prayer is that you will discern the importance of praying in the Holy Spirit.

In 2014, I was laid up in the hospital, paralyzed from the waist down to my feet. As I laid with my lower body paralyzed and extremely limited movement in my upper body; I was so weak and lifeless. The fact is the team of seven doctors who had placed me in the neurological intensive unit was disturbed about the guillain-barré syndrome that had already induced paralysis in my legs and was working its way up to my lungs and heart which brought me into a near death position. Yes, I was literally on my death bed, There were times I would come in and out of the conscious state—sometimes it would be the day, at times it would be the night. There was no regular

Spiritual Pursuit

pattern or schedule to it. Many times, I found myself so weak but having just enough strength to pray in the Holy Spirit. Knowing that God was not going to leave me nor forsake me, I took great relief. But little did I know the power of things unfolding from the times I would pray in the Spirit. After I got out of the hospital, my spiritual mother, Momma Mig, told me of being massively influenced one night to pray for me by the Holy Spirit. I believe this was in a response of one of my moments of greatest weakness. I was at the doorway of death. She interceded, and the Lord began to reveal to her visions of Him raising me from the grave. In fact, He showed her eight different visions of Him lifting me out of the grave. That very morning, at 4 am, an angel entered my room and asked if I would like the blinds open. As the angel opened my blinds, I slipped back asleep to awaken later to a sunny morning. I had the feeling of death all over my body. I fell back asleep to awaken again and witnessing a mighty storm outside where the rain was falling sideways. And I knew in the depth of my spirit that there was a battle taking place over my life at that very moment. As I went back to sleep again, I awakened later with a beautiful sunny day again, and the very death that had held my body was broken off. I knew victory had manifested. My question is this: Had I not been praying in the Spirit when I was so weak, would the Lord have impressed my spiritual mother in such a significant time on my behalf to pray and decree? But

Day Twenty-Seven

what if she had not heard the demand and the need that very day. There's power in praying in the Spirit. I had such a tremendous faith in knowing there was an unfolding as I prayed in the Spirit and trusting God.

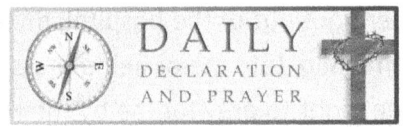

Father God, in Jesus' Name, I thank you today for the precious Holy Spirit. I thank you for bringing me to a place Lord of being baptized in the Holy Spirit with evidence of speaking in tongues because I acknowledge this is crucial and beneficial in my life with you. Lord, I desire to pray in the Spirit to see powerful things unfold for your glory. I thank you for a great awakening inside of me, a deeper place with the Holy Spirit in tongues. I acknowledge to you. I don't need my own understanding in this; I need your Spirit, Lord. And I desire this day to be filled and pray in the Spirit all the days of my life and see mighty accomplishments and miracles take place, in Jesus' Name, Amen!

DAY TWENTY-EIGHT

DESIRE GREATER WISDOM

To one is given the word of wisdom through the Spirit.
1 Corinthians 12:8

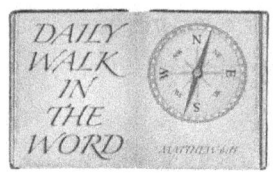

1 Corinthians 2:6-16

Day Twenty-Eight

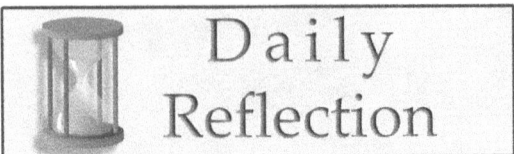
Daily Reflection

God has given us gifts to advance the Kingdom of God and make us powerful, and productive in that. We are to desire the greatest gifts. And one of these gifts is the gift of wisdom—yes, the very word of wisdom! So many times, we are met with decisions; sometimes a business choice on what needs to be done to advance the business, or to do something new. God desires to help us. He's there to speak to us as long as our priorities are aligned with His.

The very word of wisdom is meant for a time that you're under a lot of pressure concerning something God has put before you to accomplish. Again, whether that is a business transaction, or whether that is something to do with your church, or even in your family, there are times you will need to obtain a word of wisdom.

Many times, in our journey, we've talked about the importance of being filled with the Holy Spirit, and we are to desire the gifts of the Spirit. As we are filled with the Holy Spirit, He can come and manifest any other gifts at any time in us. Remember, the Bible tells us to desire

Spiritual Pursuit

earnestly the best gifts that we can advance the Kingdom of God take a look at 1 Corinthians 14:1

Today, sit down and pray and ask God what you need, what gift you need. Begin to press in and come to know His voice better and better every day and every way. Remember, He desires to grant us these great gifts. So today, I encourage you to believe and receive and to not be afraid to ask Him for the best gifts.

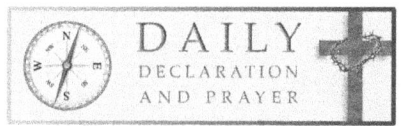

Father God, in Jesus' Name, guide me Lord to the gifts I need today. In Jesus' name, Amen!

DAY TWENTY-NINE

THE POWER OF FAITH

Above all, taking the shield of faith with which you will be able to quench all the fiery darts of the wicked one.
Ephesians 6:16

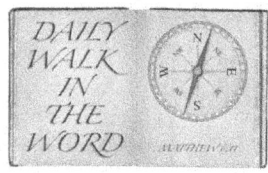

Hebrews 11:1-3

Day Twenty-Nine

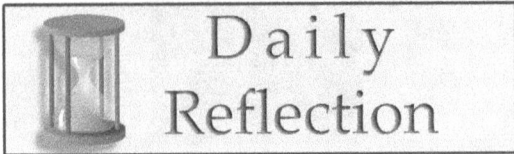
Daily Reflection

In my walk with God, there have been many times that situations arose and I was going to have to have tremendous faith to overcome. In fact, some of those times, it was like it went deeper than my faith existed. And many times, I cried out to the Lord, and His grace surfaced, and my faith increased.

There have been many times in my walk that I had nothing: no checking account, no savings account, not a dime, but I had the Lord. He always provided what I needed when I needed it. The actuality is, the Lord is always going to meet us when we're living and walking in a great place of faith, almost like walking on the edge of a building and trusting the Lord.

No matter what you're facing today, it's time to go to the edge of trusting God. It's time to make that request before the Lord and cry out to Him. It's time to have the faith to know that His trust is real and that we can trust Him. Let it all go. Press into the Spirit. Rise up to that place of great glory in the Lord and let God take those

Spiritual Pursuit

challenges and pour out every desire that you bring to Him.

Remember, there is no end with God. The limit is within us. With God, all things are possible. Each time we grow in faith—that is, face a situation that seems too hard, too distant, and yet He shows up time and time again in His perfect time—we grow to a more profound place of genuinely having limitless faith.

Embrace the journey and go forth as God continues to show you the enormous power of faith.

Day Twenty-Nine

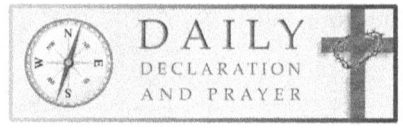

Father God, in Jesus' Name, I come boldly before you today and release it all to you, pressing into a greater place with your Spirit, into a higher place of faith, God, to see time and time again your hand show up in my situation. I thank you, Lord, today that you're meeting each challenge, Father, and pouring out the desires of my heart and taking me to even a greater place of limitless faith in you, Lord God. In Jesus' Name, Amen!

DAY THIRTY

THE GIFT OF FAITH

But one and the same Spirit works all these things,
distributing to each one individually as He wills.
1 Corinthians 12:11

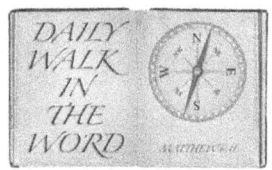

Ephesians 3

Day Thirty-One

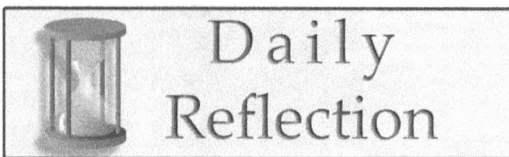
Daily Reflection

A lot of times we've talked about the gifts of God and many times the gift of faith. We are to desire the gifts because the gifts are important but even more important than having the gifts is daily making our advancement in God. Yes, our every decision, our every choice, our every step!

Many times, in the Bible, we will see that the realities of our life grow daily. In other words, what happened today may be greater in the place of reality than what took place yesterday. Remember, in God; nothing is dead, barren, or dry in this life because Jesus came to give life through the Holy Spirit.

God's always doing something for us, but we've got to make a daily advancement with Him either moving ahead or backsliding. That's the simple look of it.

There have been times when the Holy Spirit's moved upon me in great faith. I've noticed somebody walking down the street, He'd reveal to me where they required a healing or had a problem, and I would step out in great

Spiritual Pursuit

faith and approach them and ask them, "The Lord has revealed this or revealed that to me. Can I pray for you?" And many times His love and concern overtake them, they're okay with receiving prayer and healing.

The reality is, every time they opened up for it, God showed up, and the people were immediately healed, set free of their pain. When we're truly operating in the Holy Spirit and the gift that He's given us, we are connected to Him because He is the One doing it.

The gift of faith is a significant and very important gift.

In Matthew 12:13, He told the man to stretch out his hand. He had faith to tell him to do that. He had faith to believe and trust God and when He did, what happened? Something was spoken, and something took place. It was accomplished.

You must be broken before the Lord, humble before the Lord, and submitted. At that point, God can trust you with the gifts to respond in faith and move as He'd have us to do.

Day Thirty-One

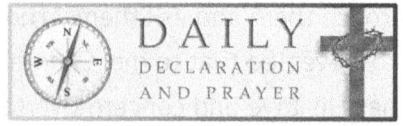

Father God, in Jesus' Name, I thank you, Lord, for a broken and contrite spirit. I thank you for faith, God, to step out, Lord, by your Holy Spirit and meet the needs, Father, of those in my community and around the world. Lord, I thank you for today and the gift of faith, God, in my life increasing, in Jesus' Name.

DAY THIRTY-ONE

THE BAPTISM IN THE SPIRIT

Acts 2:4
And they were all filled with the Holy Spirit and began to speak with other tongues, as the Spirit gave them utterance.

Acts 2: 1-18

Day Thirty-One

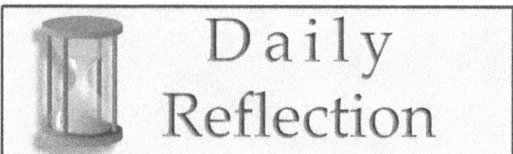
Daily Reflection

We have had an extraordinary 31-day journey going to deeper places in the Holy Spirit, and now we have significant life-changing news: If you have not already received the Holy Spirit here is your opportunity.

To obtain the Baptism of the Holy Spirit, it is as simple as asking your heavenly Father for the baptism in the Holy Spirit. God wants each believer to desire and be filled with the precious Holy Spirit and to speak in His spiritual language of unknown tongues.

In the book of Acts 2: 4 they were all filled with the Holy Spirit and began to speak with other tongues, as the Spirit gave them utterance. Now let's take a look at Acts 10: 38 we see He anointed His children with the Holy Spirit and with power, and this is so we will go about doing good, and healing all who are oppressed by the devil; because He is always with us. Next, let us look at Luke 3:16 "I baptize you with water. But one more powerful than I will come, the thongs of whose sandals I am not worthy to untie. He will baptize you with the Holy Spirit and with fire.

Spiritual Pursuit

Are you ready?
First. Just Ask God now.
Second have faith and receive the Baptism of the Holy Spirit, by believing God's Word. We are His children, and as our Father, He is thrilled and eager to baptize each of us in His precious Holy Spirit. When you ask Him, you will receive.

Pray this prayer and believe in faith.
Father God, I come to You now in my Lord and Savior Jesus Christ name, and I proceed to You in one accord in the Name of Jesus. I plead the Blood of Jesus Christ over me and say thanks for the most incredible gift of salvation in Jesus Christ. Lord, You guaranteed me the free gift of the Holy Spirit, and I am asking You, to baptize and fill me with Your precious Holy Spirit, just as You baptized and filled Your disciples at Pentecost. Breathe into me the precious Holy Spirit. Thank You that You restore, strengthen and reinforce me with the tremendous power of the Holy Spirit. Thank You, Lord Jesus, that I am filled with the Holy Spirit and speak with other tongues, as the Spirit gives us utterance.

That's it! You have received the Baptism in the Holy Spirit!

Day Thirty-One

Now it's possible you didn't feel anything. In some cases, no new language comes out initially. But your receiving the Holy Spirit has nothing to do with initial feelings or what happens on the outside.

God's Word said that if you asked, you would receive. That means by faith you have received the Baptism in the Holy Spirit. Practice speaking in other tongues. It doesn't matter if you begin with one syllable or how silly you appear. Merely keep praying, and God will strengthen you in your prayer language. Many people receive the Baptism in the Holy Spirit and do not pray in tongues right away. Don't be discouraged; it will develop and grow. Just don't give up!

Spiritual Pursuit

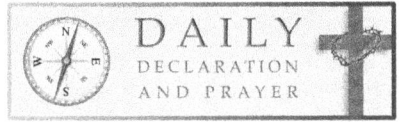

Father God, in the mighty name of the Lord Jesus' Christ, I thank you for this 31-day journey to a deeper and more powerful walk with you in your precious Holy Spirit. O declare and decree that from this day forward I will never be the same in Jesus Christ name. Lord, I desire to be you obedient laid down lover to go forth and heal the sick, cast out devils and set the captives free and through the power and gifts of the Holy Spirit this day I am walking into the fullness In Jesus' Name, Amen!

Ministry Contact

Lead by Faith Ministries, Inc.
LBFWorld
P.O. Box 1198
Porter, TX 77365
844.523.9531
LBFWorld.com
info@lbfworld.com

RichardbSimmons.com

Twitter / Instagram
Twitter: @richardbsimmons
Instagram: @therichardbsimmons

Television
watch.hourisnow.tv
HisPresenceTv.com
HisTouchNetwork.com

Facebook
Spiritual Pursuit Book

Richard invites you to his journey of coming out of darkness into the light in his amazon best selling book The Miracle Child

The *Miracle Child Book* is a story full of hope, light and positivity that will guide you to a place of love, hope and happiness. A place of comfort and harmony.

Learn how Jesus Christ can work in your life and embark on this journey of personal transformation with the help of The *Miracle Child Book*

Miraclechildbook.com

"The miracle child is an excellent depiction of Gods unconditional love, grace and mercy."
-T R C

"I wanted to know how one could overcome all of the obstacles, barriers and hardships endured through life, as Richard has!"
-Linda B

"This book will breathe life into the person that needs their next breath to move forward in life!"
-Carol B

View Richard's other writing

Amazon Author Page

Barnes & Nobles

Jet Books

LBFWorld Publishing

www.ingramcontent.com/pod-product-compliance
Lightning Source LLC
Chambersburg PA
CBHW071459070426
42452CB00041B/1935